HELPING TRAUMATIZED FAMILIES

Charles R. Figley

HELPING TRAUMATIZED FAMILIES

 Jossey-Bass Publishers

San Francisco • Oxford • 1989

HELPING TRAUMATIZED FAMILIES
by Charles R. Figley

Copyright © 1989 by: Jossey-Bass Inc., Publishers
350 Sansome Street
San Francisco, California 94104
&
Jossey-Bass Limited
Headington Hill Hall
London OX3 0BW

Library of Congress Cataloging-in-Publication Data

Figley, Charles R., date.
    Helping traumatized families / Charles R. Figley. — 1st ed.
        p.   cm. — (The Jossey-Bass social and behavioral science
series)
    Bibliography: p.
    Includes index.
    ISBN 1-55542-189-X (alk. paper)
    1. Family psychotherapy. I. Title. II. Series.
    [DNLM: 1. Family Therapy—methods. 2. Stress Disorders, Post
 Traumatic—therapy. WM 170 F472h]
RC488.5.F54   1989
616.89′156—dc20   89-15543
                                                        CIP

Manufactured in the United States of America

The paper in this book meets the guidelines for
permanence and durability of the Committee on
Production Guidelines for Book Longevity of the
Council on Library Resources.

JACKET DESIGN BY WILLI BAUM

FIRST EDITION

Code 8962

The Jossey-Bass
Social and Behavioral Science Series

To the memory of my father
John David Figley

CONTENTS

PREFACE

How would you feel if you and your family were suddenly struggling with a situation you had never thought was possible? For example, how would you cope if your child were diagnosed with an incurable disease that left you and your family devastated, angry, confused, and hopeless? Perhaps you and your family have already experienced times of chaos and disillusionment, though they may not have lasted very long. Those of us who have experienced such times struggle along as best we can, not sure that we are coping as well as we might.

For nearly two decades I have worked with traumatized families dealing with a variety of stressful situations. My successes have outnumbered my failures, but there clearly were failures, particularly in the beginning.

I began to write this book in 1972, soon after my first professional work with a traumatized family. I am not sure why it has taken so long to complete it. Perhaps it is because I did not have enough to say until now or perhaps because I failed miserably with that first client family and have never quite recovered from it—I was traumatized, as it were.

Completing this book ends what has been for me quite a long and, at times, lonely journey. It began with a personal concern for the welfare of the families of American veterans of the Vietnam War, shifted to a concentration on the families of

Americans held hostage in Iran, and expanded to include an examination of families exposed to a variety of catastrophes: natural and man-made disasters, criminal assaults, inter- and intrafamily abuse, death, and terminal illness.

Now that I have completed the book I can turn my attention more fully to other issues and topics that also capture my attention. But none will ever be more important to me than my interest in families struggling to overcome memories of horror. I hope I have made at least a small contribution toward the alleviation of their suffering.

Overview of the Contents

In writing *Helping Traumatized Families* I hoped to fulfill at least three objectives: (1) to review what we know about traumatized families, including definitions of some important concepts and several theoretical models that clarify them; (2) to discuss the ways families typically cope with trauma, including both functional and dysfunctional patterns of coping; and (3) to describe a comprehensive approach to treating traumatized families. The book's content is consistent with these objectives.

In Chapter One I focus on how and why I view families as systems of interacting relationships. I expand on this perspective in the next several chapters by describing the building blocks of my theory of traumatized family processes. Also in the first chapter I define what I mean by trauma and who I believe constitute "traumatized families." I continue in Chapter One to emphasize the universality of trauma—many more people, and thus families, are traumatized than we once thought.

In Chapter Two I address the second objective of the book. I note how important families are to all of us and show how families have natural and remarkably effective ways of helping traumatized members (detecting traumatic stress, urging confrontation of the stressor, urging recapitulation of the catastrophe, and facilitating resolution of the conflicts). I also review the ways in which families are naturally supportive of their members. Indeed, families are so effective and efficient in helping traumatized members that I have tailored my approach to treating families on the basis of these naturally existing methods. These methods include clarifying insights, correcting distortions, and supporting alternative perspectives.

In Chapter Two I introduce a way of summarizing the powerful role families play in human functioning and the process by which the family system confronts and recovers from trauma. This family adaptation model incorporates research from many studies of families exposed to highly stressful experiences. Chapter Two provides a context that conveys an appreciation of the variety of ways in which families cope with stressors and clarifies the characteristics that differentiate functional from dysfunctional family coping.

The remaining chapters address the third objective of the book. In Chapter Three I present the theoretical building blocks for my approach to conceptualizing, assessing, and treating traumatized families. In my work I attempt to empower the family members to make peace with the past and take charge of their lives. This kind of intervention could be categorized as primary as well as secondary prevention. In addition to helping families make peace with the past, I educate them about trauma, traumatic stress, family functioning, and recovery. Moreover, I attempt to enhance their natural resources, including their basic family social skills and supportiveness.

In Chapter Four I present my approach to evaluating the family system client, beginning with a detailed description of the clinical interview, and then describe several useful standardized measures of stress, traumatic stress, social support, and family pathology.

The remainder of the book focuses on the empowerment approach to helping traumatized families. In Chapter Five I describe and justify the eight basic clinical objectives for helping traumatized families and include a detailed description of my five-phase approach to empowering traumatized families.

In Chapters Six through Ten I describe each of these phases in detail: Phase One (Chapter Six) is building commitment to the therapeutic objectives, Phase Two (Chapter Seven) is framing the problem, Phase Three (Chapter Eight) is reframing the problem, Phase Four (Chapter Nine) is developing a healing

theory, and Phase Five (Chapter Ten) is closure and preparedness.

Chapter Eleven is devoted entirely to a discussion of helping traumatized children, beginning with a section focusing on
developmental issues and including a list of children's methods
for coping with trauma. Most of the chapter, however, focuses
on methods useful in helping children within a family context.

In the final chapter, Chapter Twelve, I return to my objectives for the book in an effort to summarize the major points.
I also discuss the special nature of traumatized families, the
emerging field that specializes in their study and care, and the
special challenges to research, treatment, and the practitioner in
working with this special population.

Included as resources at the end of the book are three
questionnaires. The Traumagram Questionnaire (Resource A)
and the Purdue Post-Traumatic Stress Disorder Scale (Resource
B) are useful in identifying the existence and severity of traumatic events. The Purdue Social Support Scale (Resource C) can
help the practitioner to assess the quality and quantity of social
support among client family members.

Audience

I wrote *Helping Traumatized Families* with practitioners
in mind—those who struggle on a regular basis to help families,
particularly traumatized families: psychologists, psychiatrists
and other physicians, nurses, clergy, social workers, and family
therapists. If the book fulfills my intended goals, it will become
a primary resource for identifying and assisting individuals and
families coping with trauma. A secondary audience may be students being trained to work with traumatized families or individuals.

Thus it is my hope that this book will become the primary reference for the assessment and treatment of those traumatized by a wide variety of stressors. I hope it will help practitioners identify, empathize with, and generally understand
traumatized individuals and families and the interactions among
family members.

Academic readers (especially students) will be more interested in the first half of the book, which focuses on the scientific literature and description of the problem. Indeed, this book draws on the separate literatures of cognitive and behavioral psychology, crisis intervention, traumatic stress, family therapy, disaster/traumatic stress, and community mental health in general. However, this book fits well within the growing area of specialization on family stress and coping.

Mostly, I hope that this book will provide a sense of inspiration and motivation for working with frightened and confused people, those traumatized by one or more circumstances. The book emerged from my experiences with hundreds of traumatized people and families. Out of their lives and their courage emerged a perspective that has helped me help them. At the same time, they have given me an appreciation of their special struggles and extraordinary achievements.

Dedication

This book is dedicated to my father, John David Figley, who died in 1981 at the age of fifty-six and, in so doing, left his wife and two children a traumatized family. His sudden illness and death challenged us to draw together for strength and courage and, in the process, provided considerable insight into the experiences of traumatized families. My love for him permeates every page of this book and the years required to write it.

Acknowledgments

This book would still be in process were it not for Gracia A. Alkema of Jossey-Bass. Her persistence in seeking my commitment to complete the book and her gentle encouragement were helpful and are appreciated. The three reviewers hired by Jossey-Bass—Will A. Kouw, Pennie Myers, and Constance Hoenk Shapiro—were especially helpful in suggesting ways to reshape the final manuscript.

My colleagues at Purdue University, particularly the members of the clinical marriage and family therapy faculty—Wallace

Denton, Don Hartsough, Thorana Nelson, Fred Piercy, and Douglas Sprenkle—were a constant source of encouragement. My doctoral students interested in this area over recent years were also an inspiration. They were Sandra Burge, Kathleen Gilbert, Chrys Harris, Richard Kishur, Walter Schumm, Shirley Ann Segal, William Southerly, and Robert Stretch.

Finally, my immediate family were much more patient and encouraging than I deserve. Thanks to my wife, Marilyn G. Reeves, and two daughters, Jessica and Laura.

Tallahassee, Florida   Charles R. Figley
August 1989

THE AUTHOR

Charles R. Figley is a professor of family therapy and since July 1989 has served jointly as director of the Psychosocial Stress Research Program in the School of Social Work and director of the interdivisional Ph.D. program in marriage and family therapy, all at Florida State University. Prior to that, he was professor of family therapy and psychology at Purdue University. He is a fellow and approved supervisor of the American Association for Marriage and Family Therapy and a fellow of both the American Orthopsychiatric Association and the American Psychological Association.

Figley received his B.S. degree (1970) in human development from the University of Hawaii and both his M.S. degree (1971) in human development and his Ph.D. degree (1974) in human development from Pennsylvania State University. Since then, in addition to being elected to the boards of directors of numerous national professional organizations, he has served as founding president of the Society for Traumatic Stress Studies, president of the Groves Conference on Marriage and the Family, and vice-president for publications of the National Council on Family Relations. He is also a candidate for president-elect of the American Psychological Association's Division 43, Family Psychology.

Figley has authored or edited over one hundred scholarly

papers and ten books, including *Stress Disorders Among Vietnam Veterans: Theory, Research, and Treatment* (1978), *Trauma and Its Wake: The Study and Treatment of Post-Traumatic Stress Disorder* (1985), *Trauma and Its Wake: Vol. 2. Post-Traumatic Stress Disorder: Theory, Research, and Treatment* (1986), and *Treating Stress in Families* (1989). He has been founding editor of the *Journal of Psychotherapy and the Family* since 1984 and of the international *Journal of Traumatic Stress* since 1987. He also serves as consulting editor for five other scholarly journals.

HELPING TRAUMATIZED FAMILIES

CHAPTER 1

Understanding
Traumatized Families

Case of the Murray Family

Mary Murray (all names here are fictitious) was jolted from
her thoughts by a co-worker's announcement: "Mary, Tammy's
principal needs to speak with you right away." Mr. Perez informed Mary that her eleven-year-old daughter had been overheard saying she was planning to commit suicide.

After consultation with the school counselor, Tammy
was referred to a local psychotherapist for evaluation. After one
session with the therapist, it was recommended that the rest of
the family join her: her parents, John and Mary, and her nine-
year-old brother, Tim. The clinician determined that Tammy
was under considerable stress from the pressures of school and
home. At the same time the clinician hypothesized that the
family was in a state of shock, traumatized by a series of stressful jolts that had been building for months and were now culminating in Tammy's suicide talk.

John, the father, had recently sought treatment for "exhaustion," although by all previous indications he had been the
model of a happy and productive executive. But in the last six
weeks his life had been in shambles. He had been able to sleep
only a few hours each night. He had missed more work this past
month (because of various minor illnesses) than at any time in

1

his life. He felt jumpy and irritable and fluctuated between feeling apathetic and enraged. According to Mary, his wife of fifteen years, he was no longer interested in the things that once brought him joy: his children, Little League coaching, fishing, and photography.

What was most troublesome to John, however, was his re-experiencing of several troubling memories of past events. These events had occurred over fifteen years ago when he was a corpsman in the war in Vietnam. Although he had not thought much about the war since returning home, he was now experiencing both daydreams and nightmares of the war almost daily. He had tried to talk about these experiences with Mary. She listened and tried to encourage John to put his memories behind him for the good of his family and himself. He tried to forget the past but could not. Moreover, he was unable to recall certain periods of time during his year-long tour of duty in the war. He was frightened, confused, and concerned that his boss and co-workers would think he was unable to function effectively in his extremely responsible position.

In the last few years Mary had threatened divorce, was frequently depressed, had difficulty sleeping, and was probably abusing alcohol. Both Tim and Tammy had been extremely upset and were more and more depressed about what had been happening to their family. They both were doing poorly in school, tending to avoid being at home with their father, and fighting among themselves more frequently. Both felt that if they were better children, they could help their family and parents out of this situation.

The family had struggled along this way for weeks, until Tammy's depression led to her thoughts about suicide. The family assembled for treatment, at first to focus their attention on correcting Tammy's depression. Soon, however, they would be dealing with other stressors that had culminated in a traumatized family.

Fortunately, the clinician was able to see beyond Tammy's suicide talk to recognize that it might be symptomatic of a traumatized family. Clinicians trained to work with *individual* trauma victims have many models to guide their interventions (see Figley, 1978, 1985b, 1986b; Horowitz, 1986; Ochberg, 1988). Yet the family system as illustrated by the Murray family requires attention, even though much of the trauma can be traced to the father's experiences and in particular to the family's reactions to his efforts to handle his memories.

I have worked with traumatized families for over fifteen years and have felt their pain, marveled at their resilience, and celebrated with them as they recovered. As with so many families, the Murrays' struggles are easy to see but are much more complex and effectively helped when viewed in a broader context.

As stated in the preface, I have three main objectives: (1) to review what we know about traumatized families, including definitions of some important concepts and several theoretical models that clarify them; (2) to discuss the typical ways families cope with trauma, including both functional and dysfunctional patterns of coping; and (3) to describe a comprehensive approach to treating a variety of traumatized families.

In this chapter you will see that there are many more traumatized families than most people realize. These families are often not noticed. Most often they are viewed as the "victim's family." In the last decade human service systems have recognized that unless we attend to the social network of the victim, the victim will not recover quickly from her or his stressful experiences. Yet, as a result of the traumatic experiences, the network (most often the "victim" is the family) can barely handle routine matters and may be unable to help members struggling to recover emotionally.

I hope that this book will provide a way to view and help *both* the traumatized person and the traumatized family (or other social system). Certainly it is common for the family or another family member to be *responsible* for the trauma, as in the case of incest. Sometimes the abused family member may be the only person who is traumatized in the family. These unfortunate cases will be addressed later. The bulk of the material in this book, however, focuses on the *system* of the *traumatized* family and on how best to detect and help these families.

In this chapter I introduce my perspectives on helping traumatized families: the meaning of a systems perspective on the family and the meaning of trauma and traumatized families. Later I discuss my theory and practice of helping, or *empowering*, traumatized people in families. Let us start with some definitions.

Viewing Families as Systems

Much of my graduate training and professional work over the last two decades involved viewing families as systems. A dictionary definition of a system is "a regularly interacting or interdependent group of items forming a unified whole." There are many examples of systems that are directly analogous to a family system. The human body is a biological system with different organs with different functions that must work together in concert. An orchestra is a system with different instruments played together for a particular sound. These systems have separate parts with varying functions that all must work together for a desired outcome. So it is with families.

Those of us with a systems perspective always view individuals within a social context, most often involving the family. Viewing families as systems involves recognizing that the relationships formed among family members are extremely powerful and account for a considerable amount of human behavior, emotion, values, and attitudes. Moreover, like strands of a spiderweb, each family relationship, as well as each family member, influences all other family relationships and all other family members.

(Many term-laden systemic concepts have emerged over the years, particularly in family therapy theory, to identify the various components and functions within the family system. I have consciously tried to avoid such terms and other professional jargon. In addition to wanting to write the most coherent book possible, I also wish to write one that appeals to colleagues from various disciplines, theoretical orientations, cultures, and languages. Making it as easy as possible for them to read this book outweighs the potential criticism of family therapy colleagues and others who specialize in either families or traumatized stress.)

Viewing Traumatized Families. The connectedness of family members with one another is why they are so vulnerable to stress, particularly traumatic stress. When one person in a family—or any semiclosed system, such as a fraternity or sorority, a card club, or a submarine crew—is upset, this upset is sensed by others in the system. Almost immediately efforts are made to correct the problem: reduce the stress, eliminate the stressor, find an effective coping method. So it is with traumatized families.

Traumatized families are those who are attempting to cope with an extraordinary stressor that has disrupted their normal life routine in unwanted ways. Relying on the dictionary once again, trauma is defined as "an injury (as a wound) to living tissue caused by an extrinsic agent; disordered psychic or behavioral state resulting from mental or emotional stress or physical injury." The analogy of a physical wound is not always directly applicable to either people or systems such as families, yet it is a useful metaphor for appreciating the process by which we respond to particular stressors over many years.

A traumatized family, then, is struggling to recover from, to cope with, an injury or wound to their system. As will be noted later, this "injury" can happen in many different ways and at various levels of intensity. The "injury" could range from a seemingly small incident that would be a minor annoyance to another family to the death or extraordinary abuse of one or more family members. What is most critical, however, is the fact that the trauma experienced by one family member may be experienced by the entire family system.

I thus define traumatized families as those who were exposed to a stressor that resulted in unwanted disruptions in their life routine. As noted above, the "injury" or stressor could be any one of a large number of events or series of events. As will be noted later, the most critical issue is the beliefs, points of view, perceptions, frames of reference, or cognitive appraisals of family members—both separately and collectively.

Post-Traumatic Stress and Stress Disorders. One important sub-set of traumatized families are those with at least one member who is suffering from Post-Traumatic Stress Disorder (PTSD). This disorder is characterized by a set of symptoms that are noted in Table 1. These include but are not limited to experi-

Table 1. Diagnostic Criteria for Post-Traumatic Stress Disorder.

309.89 Post-Traumatic Stress Disorder

A. The person has experienced an event that is outside the range of usual human experience and that would be markedly distressing to almost anyone, e.g., serious threat to one's life or physical integrity; serious threat or harm to one's children, spouse, or other close relatives and friends; sudden destruction of one's home or community; or seeing another person who has recently been, or is being, seriously injured or killed as the result of an accident or physical violence.

B. The traumatic event is persistently reexperienced in at least one of the following ways:

　　1. recurrent and intrusive distressing recollections of the event (in young children, repetitive play in which themes or aspects of the trauma are expressed)
　　2. recurrent distressing dreams of the event
　　3. sudden acting or feeling as if the traumatic event were recurring (includes a sense of reliving the experience, illusions, hallucinations, and dissociative [flashback] episodes, even those that occur upon awakening or when intoxicated)
　　4. intense physiological distress at exposure to events that symbolize or resemble an aspect of the traumatic event, including anniversaries of the trauma

C. Persistent avoidance of stimuli associated with the trauma or numbing of responsiveness (not present before the trauma), as indicated by at least two of the following:

　　1. efforts to avoid thoughts or feelings associated with the trauma
　　2. efforts to avoid activities or situations that arouse recollections of the trauma
　　3. inability to recall an important aspect of the trauma (psychogenic amnesia)
　　4. markedly diminished interest in significant activities (in young children, loss of recently acquired developmental skills such as toilet training or language skills)
　　5. feeling of detachment or estrangement from others
　　6. restricted range of affect, e.g., unable to have loving feelings
　　7. sense of a foreshortened future, e.g., child does not expect to have a career, marriage, or children, or a long life

Table 1. Diagnostic Criteria for Post-Traumatic Stress Disorder, Cont'd.

D. Persistent symptoms of increased arousal (not present before the trauma) as indicated by at least two of the following:

    1. difficulty falling or staying asleep
    2. irritability or outburst of anger
    3. difficulty concentrating
    4. hypervigilance
    5. exaggerated startle response
    6. physiologic reactivity upon exposure to events that symbolize or resemble an aspect of the traumatic event (e.g., a woman who was raped in an elevator breaks out in a sweat when entering any elevator)

E. Duration of disturbance (symptoms in B, C, and D) of at least one month.

Specify delayed onset if the onset of symptoms was at least six months after the trauma.

Source: Reprinted with permission from the *Diagnostic and Statistical Manual of Mental Disorders, Third Edition, Revised.* Copyright 1987 American Psychiatric Association.

encing recurrent nightmares, intrusive thoughts, or flashbacks of a traumatic event; phobic behavior or generalized apathy; and hypervigilance and other symptoms of increased arousal lasting longer than one month. Some clients experience bouts of amnesia surrounding the traumatizing experience or catastrophe. After an acute phase that includes exhibiting traumatic stress reactions, such as anxiety symptoms, clients who develop PTSD tend also to display symptoms of depression, somatic symptoms, and, for some, antisocial or sociopathic tendencies.

As we will discuss in the next chapter, PTSD occurs after a highly stressful event or series of events. These events are considered outside the usual range of human experiences and would be distressing to almost anyone. What would be "traumatic" includes exposure to various life-threatening events, such as a fire, bad traffic accident, natural or man-made disaster, war, or train or airplane crash, or criminal victimization, such as rape and other violent acts.

Although most individuals correctly associate their PTSD symptoms with the catastrophe they experienced, some may be unable to make the connection. This may be due to some need to deny the event and the suffering it caused. For example, those traumatized in the performance of their duty (for example, firefighters, police officers, or emergency medical personnel) may be quite reluctant to admit that they have developed PTSD symptoms for fear of losing their job or being perceived as unfit for duty. Others may be unable to make the connection between symptoms and their past experiences due to amnesia, blocking the entire traumatic memory or key elements of the event. For those with physical injuries or who are preoccupied with those of loved ones or busy rebuilding a home following a catastrophe, the psychological symptoms may either go unnoticed, or the onset of symptoms may be delayed for months or years.

In the acute phase of PTSD, symptoms associated with anxiety tend to predominate, as do startle responses, intrusive thoughts, flashbacks of the incident, and sleeping problems. Sometimes PTSD sufferers recover, in part with the help of social supporters, particularly family members. However, some PTSD cases become either delayed in onset or chronic. Here the symptoms become more problematical and antisocial: despondency, depression, dampening of affect, sexual dysfunction, somatic symptoms, and efforts to avoid reminders of the traumatic event become more evident.

But just how many people have actually experienced such extraordinary stressors, either directly or indirectly, through family and close friends?

Unfortunately, studies that assess the prevalence of a highly stressful event in the general population are rare. One important exception is a study by Russell (1984, 1986). The sample included 930 adult women who were randomly selected and interviewed. Russell found that 24 percent of the sample survived at least one rape in their life, and 31 percent reported at least one experience of attempted rape. Moreover, Russell found in her study that 14 percent of the married women reported a sexual assault by their husband. Limiting incidence to only the last twelve months, she found that approximately 3.5 percent of these women were raped by their husbands, more than seven times higher than the 0.5 percent figure published by the National Crime Survey (U.S. Department of Justice, Federal Bureau of Investigation, 1986). Russell notes that assuming this rate remains the same, American women have nearly a 50 percent chance of being raped at some time in their life.

Childhood sexual abuse figures, although lower, are still alarming. According to Russell, 16 percent of her sample had been sexually abused by a blood relative, and 31 percent reported at least one experience of sexual abuse by a nonrelative before the age of eighteen. This is consistent with Herman's (1981) landmark report of five studies between 1940 and 1975. Together these studies showed that between 20 percent and 33 percent of all women report an unwanted childhood sexual encounter with an adult male blood relative.

Koss, Gidycz, and Wisniewski (1987) found, among a national sample of 3,187 college women, that 27.5 percent reported being a victim of rape or an attempted rape *after* the age of fourteen. Moreover, 14 percent of the married women in this student sample reported a sexual assault by their husband.

In terms of criminal victimization, Herrington (1985) reports that 37 million Americans were victims of crime in 1984. This number includes 6 million victims of *violent* crime.

Perhaps the most comprehensive study of community mental health ever conducted was recently reported in the *New England Journal of Medicine* (Schlenger et al., in press). This was a congressionally mandated epidemiological study of randomly selected households throughout the United States. The study focused on the Vietnam War generation in an effort to determine the prevalence rate of PTSD among those who served in Vietnam versus among those who did not. The findings indicated that 15.2 percent of the Vietnam veteran group had the disorder at the time of the survey, and 22.5 percent (males) and 21.2 percent (females) of Vietnam veterans at some time in their life. These rates are about six times higher than the rates for their non–Vietnam veteran peers.

Another recent study was not limited to focusing on mental health problems, including PTSD. A recent study (Segal & Figley, 1988) suggests that our estimates of the frequency with which individuals are exposed to highly stressful events may be too low. In the process of developing an inventory for measuring traumatic stress vulnerability, they found that 80 percent (225 of the 281 respondents) of a "low-risk population" (a representative sample of undergraduates from an introductory psychology course at Purdue University) had experienced a highly stressful event.

Unfortunately, figures on the frequency of other, often less traumatizing events are unavailable. Yet it is safe to say that, like the Murray family, most American families have been traumatized at some time and to some extent. Most of these families attempt to struggle through their ordeals without seeking assistance. In the following pages I try to describe the way I view these families and my approaches to assessing and helping empower them to recover from their stressful experiences and, I hope, be strong for it.

Chapter Two provides a more detailed overview of family stress and coping and how professionals can learn from what families do naturally. I always try to notice what families do well, their strengths and resources, and help them build on this base. Next I will suggest that families are experts at helping traumatized people—family members—and that, unfortunately, some family members may be experts at traumatizing.

CHAPTER 2

How Families Cope with Trauma

The Murray family and all families are fascinating systems, and, like the people who compose them, no two families are alike. To understand the best ways of helping traumatized families, indeed, any family, is to appreciate the "healing" or ameliorative potential of the system—that there is a range of coping abilities, strengths, and resource reserves in all families to recover. Our job as family specialists is to discover our family client's natural resources and what they need to mobilize these resources and manage their challenges effectively.

As I noted in the last chapter, the human body is a self-contained system able to recover from a wide variety of ailments and physical traumas, and the family system has similar capabilities. As members of a family we come to rely on and, in turn, be relied on to perform certain functions at a certain minimum level of competence under certain conditions.

For the Murray family, for example, both parents work and provide shelter, income, and protection for themselves and their children. Moreover, the parents are responsible for the reproduction, nurturance, education, and socialization of their children. The spouses rely on each other for love, companionship, friendship, sexual gratification, and general social support. The children are a source of love, encouragement, and stimulation (that is, they drive you crazy sometimes!). With so many

11

important functions being performed by so few people, it is not surprising that we are so affected and influenced by other members of our family. It is also why families are such an extraordinary source of stress production and reduction (Figley, 1983, 1988a).

How Families Help Traumatized Members

So it is with traumatic stress. Families and family members, because we care and depend on them so much, can be instrumental in creating traumatic experiences. Once confronted with traumatic experiences, family members have the ability to make the situation much worse through malice or some insensitivity. What parent of a teenager has never felt unappreciated when attempting to help with some life challenge, often accompanied with a roll of the eyes, a smile, and a patronizing "thanks anyway, Dad."

But for the most part, most families are in effect social contexts for managing the stress of their members. Indeed, as an intimate social support system, family members promote recovery in at least four separate and related ways: (1) detecting traumatic stress, (2) confronting the trauma, (3) urging the recapitulation of the catastrophe, and (4) facilitating resolution of the trauma-inducing conflicts.

Detecting Traumatic Stress. The first way families help is simply by caring enough to notice. Traumatic stress is usually first detected in families because family members know one another so well; they can notice any changes in emotion and behavior. The concept of the family is derived from the Latin term *familia*. It is the root word of familiar and literally means "household." Unlike in modern Western cultures, in earlier times a household often included many people.

Anyone bound by a household—be they tied by blood or law—becomes well aware of the habits, dispositions, and patterns of behavior of fellow inhabitants. Add to this the similarities of inherited and acquired traits of family members, and what emerges in most families is a remarkable "feel" for the normative behavior of fellow family members.

Thus, in a "healthy" family, when one family member is having a "bad" day, other family members know it immediately. When a family member has experienced a catastrophe, he or she is expected to behave differently. Even when a family member displays symptoms of post-traumatic stress disorder for which the cause may be unknown, other family members detect the changed pattern of behavior almost immediately.

Conversely, family members often ignore/accept/tolerate the behavior of family members that would appear to be a clear sign of distress to others. I once saw a teenager (call him Jimmy) because his parents were concerned that he might attempt suicide. A few minutes into the initial interview Jimmy suddenly took a deep breath, stood up, went to the window, and stared out. My mind raced through the criteria in DSM-IIIR (Diagnostic and Statistical Manual of Mental Disorders, rev. 3rd ed.) for symptoms and a possible diagnosis. Just as suddenly he returned to his seat. When he repeated this same behavior with his parents in the room, they looked at me reassuringly and whispered: "Jimmy does that. Always has when he gets tight [worried]. It settles [calms] him."

Confronting the Stressor. A second way of helping is that family members help each other face the cause of the behavior, most often the stressor or traumatic experiences. Thus, once a member's stress reactions are noticed, family members are also in a position to begin to help the stressed family member. This may be done by simply linking the apparent stress reaction to some recent event. The method of confrontation is most often tailored to the individual needs and style of the victim in a way that only another family member could know.

In Jimmy's case, one of his teachers noticed a change in his behavior: apathy, increased window watching, preoccupation. The teacher asked Jimmy what was wrong but received only genuine denials. Still concerned, the teacher wrote to Jimmy's parents and spoke to them by phone. Then Jimmy's mother baked his favorite pie and, away from everyone else, said: "James Roberts, I know there's something eating inside you, and I think I know what it is [she did not], but I want you to tell me yourself right now. And you're not leaving until you do." Jimmy then told his mother about the death of a pen pal and about his dreams and thoughts of ending his own life like his friend of many years. His mother's approach would never work with my children, but it did with Jimmy.

For other family members, a more subtle method of confrontation has proven more effective over the years. In the case of the Murray family, for example, long before they sought help from a professional psychotherapist Mrs. Murray left Mr. Murray a copy of a book about Vietnam veterans' readjustment problems after he had a week of nightmares about the war. He had responded favorably in the past to receiving from her various books and articles about problems he was facing at the time.

Urging Recapitulation of the Catastrophe. A third way that families provide social support and facilitate recovery from trauma is *assisting the traumatized member to reconsider the traumatic events: to recapitulate what happened.* This issue is very important to the recovery process.

I have noted over the years, based on my research and clinical experiences and those of my colleagues, that those struggling to recover from traumatic events appear to need to resolve five fundamental questions: (1) What happened? (2) Why did it happen? (3) Why did I and others act as we did then? (4) Why did I and others act as we did since then? (5) If something like this happened again, would I be able to cope more effectively?

In the process of recapitulation, the family member enables the victim to recall facets of the trauma that are critical in answering the other victim questions noted earlier. A student therapist I supervised had a case that illustrates this process well. It involved a couple who had suffered a late miscarriage and had sought help in recovering. They realized they needed such help only because the husband was able to help the wife talk about why she was feeling depressed lately for no apparent reason. Only through the husband's gentle encouragement did the wife slowly come to realize that she had not fully recovered from the death of their baby, though it had happened ten years earlier. She had inadvertently noticed a particular photograph of a seashore that she had stared at in the doctor's office when she was informed about the stillbirth. Her ability to link her current depression with the traumatic experience a decade earlier was directly due to her husband's expert knowledge of her and what would and would not help her.

Facilitating Resolution of the Conflicts. Finally, the fourth way families are helpful to traumatized family members is in helping the victim work through her or his traumatic memories and accompanying conflicts. Most importantly, families help victims by "reframing" or offering alternative ways of viewing the highly stressful event and the event-related consequences in a more positive or optimistic way. For example, the traumatic event was "God's test of our faith" or "it made us more aware of how other victims feel." In doing so, they help the victim formulate a "healing theory" (Figley, 1979). All five of the victim questions must be answered to the satisfaction of the victim. Most importantly, the family member serves as an effective facilitator in developing a healing theory of the entire experience, a reframing of the predicament.

Developing such a healing theory requires considerable knowledge about the victimized family member. Such knowledge is well known to fellow family members but is acquired very slowly by therapists or others attempting to assist the victim. Family members, for example, may know best whether to be active or passive, use mutual self-disclosure or not, or be confrontive or not.

At the same time, this is a point in the recovery process where many families get "stuck." They are unable to effectively utilize the information they have about the trauma and its consequences in order to resolve or eliminate the traumatic stress.

As I have noted elsewhere (Figley, 1983, 1988a, 1988c), eliminating traumatic stress involves three separate activities within families with *highly developed skills of social supportiveness.* Most families seeking or needing traumatic stress therapy are not functioning at a high level of social supportiveness. However, I believe that it is important to review these naturally occurring functions to either activate or develop them in our client families.

These social supportiveness skills include: (1) clarifying insights, (2) correcting distortions (placing blame and credit more objectively), and (3) offering or supporting new and more "generous" or accurate perspectives on the catastrophe. As will be discussed in Chapter Nine, we attempt to train families in adopting these naturally occurring family social supportiveness methods in helping fellow family members work through their traumatic experiences.

1. Clarifying insights. The first skill is the ability of family members to accurately understand a member's perspective and, in turn, explain it to him or her. In studies of successful families (McCubbin and Figley, 1983b; Figley and McCubbin, 1983; Figley, 1985a, 1986d) we found that family members were effective in helping family members, including those most troubled by highly stressful events, to clarify insights, perspectives, frameworks, and discoveries about their ordeal made by fellow family members. Moreover, family members then would refer to these clarifications later as they relate to constructing a healing theory or reframing some aspect of their experiences. This skill involves family members in listening carefully to another's views or insights in a nonjudgmental and caring manner, then succinctly paraphrasing these views for the family member in a way that demonstrates both understanding of the facts and acceptance of the feelings.

We noted in the same reports that families usually possess the capacity for coping with a wide variety of stressors. By listening carefully to what they say and feel and feeding this information back to them and helping them feed back information to each other, they are able to work through most of their traumatic experiences. Moreover, they are able to *learn from their experiences* so that they will feel more competent and confident about future challenges.

2. Correcting distortions. The second set of social supportiveness skills demonstrated in well-functioning families is the tendency to place blame and credit more objectively. These families are able to gently guide a fellow family member to view various situations from a different perspective. This is a part of what could be called basic family relations skills (Figley & McCubbin, 1983; Guerney, 1982).

Often parents show, for example, an extraordinary capacity to help their children sort out blame and credit for their actions. This may be due in part to some parents' spending more time with their children, knowing them better, and working at it more diligently (since being interpersonally skilled is more important to some than others). This expertise is quite important in helping older children and other adults sort out the stress they are experiencing.

As noted earlier, recovering from traumatic stress is the process of developing more effective methods of memory management. With regard to this skill, families enable fellow members to more effectively "manage" their memories by correcting one member's distorted views or conclusions in a way that will lead to effective recovery.

In the course of treatment a family client of mine related a story about when her mother began to recall being sexually molested by her uncle as a young girl. First her husband and then her older daughter urged her to relate the painful story. Both helped her to admit that although she had felt guilty and partially responsible for the molestation for the past quarter century, she had been an innocent, unsuspecting child, and that her uncle had committed a crime.

3. Supporting reframes. Similarly, the third set of social supportiveness skills demonstrated in well-functioning families is the ability to offer or support new and more "generous" or accurate perspectives on the impairing stress reactions (Figley, 1983). This change in perspective can involve, for example, positively connoting what has previously been viewed as negative. These new perspectives are the final major building blocks for constructing a healing theory for the family and are thus critical skills for effectively helping family members work through their traumatic experiences (Figley, 1988a).

These abilities and skills occur naturally in well-functioning families (McCubbin & Figley, 1983a). Moreover, they are the basis for my approach in helping families (Figley, 1986a,

1986c, 1986d, 1988a). The approach involves using methods found effective in other families and in enabling families to become more effective in using these systemic methods.

Cost of Caring

There is also a cost to caring. I have noted elsewhere (Figley, 1982, 1983, 1988b) that there are costs to providing social support, particularly for close family members. Indeed, as catastrophes affect individuals, so do they affect the families of these victims: such families should be viewed as the "families of catastrophe."

One of the costs of caring is that as family members attend to the pain and suffering of their loved ones, they feel pain and suffer, too (Burgess & Holmstron, 1979; Figley, 1982, 1983, 1985b, 1988a). This is not unlike the phenomenon of *couvade*, in which expectant fathers simulate the symptoms and experiences of their pregnant wives to the extent that their abdomens become swollen and they complain of diarrhea and vomiting in the absence of medical causes (cf. Rabkin & Struening, 1976). Psychosomatic medicine has reported similar phenomena: entire families developing various maladies directly associated with some family-centered upheaval such as residential mobility (Mann, 1972) or divorce (Hetherington, Cox, & Cox, 1976).

A recent incident in our household may provide a good example of the cost of caring. Our eleven-year-old daughter, Jessica, had accidentally washed one of her contact lenses down the drain. As I tried unsuccessfully to retrieve the lens and it became clear that it was lost, she began to cry. The crying quickly increased, and soon our three-year-old, Laura, began to cry, saying, "I'm so sad for my sister," sob, sob, " 'cause I love my sister." In addition to being directly affected by catastrophes as individuals, persons belonging to families with a victimized member may experience traumatic stress.

Family members may be traumatized in at least four separate ways: (1) *simultaneous effects*, as when catastrophe directly strikes the entire family (for example, fire, natural disaster, auto accident); (2) *vicarious effects,* as when a catastrophe strikes one family member with whom the family is unable to make direct contact (for example, war, coal mine accident); (3) *chiasmal effects,* as when the traumatic stress appears to "infect" other family members after they make contact with the victimized member (for example, a nightmare about snakes after a family member discloses almost being bitten by one); and (4) *intrafamilial trauma,* as when a catastrophe strikes from within the family (for example, incest, violence, divorce).

Simultaneous Effects. When families caught in natural disasters were first studied, they were expected to have major mental health problems, yet they appeared to be relatively free of disaster-related emotional difficulties (see, for example, Smith, 1983). Perhaps one of the reasons why natural disasters appear to leave so few emotional scars (see Quarantelli, 1985) is that they often strike intact social support systems such as families, neighborhoods, and communities simultaneously. Conversely, this widespread destruction is linked with considerable social and emotional disruption (Gleser, Green, & Winget, 1981). As a result, *everyone* is a fellow survivor and is able to appreciate and provide effective and knowledgeable support. There is little "blaming the victim," for example, because *everyone in the family* is a victim. Families affected simultaneously by disaster are able to help each other to overcome the emotional horrors, to rebuild, and to recognize any valuable lessons that can be learned. Catastrophe-related pathology is less frequent in these situations than in the others.

Vicarious Effects. In contrast, when we learn by some medium (for example, telephone, television, letter) that a catastrophe has affected someone we love, this is extremely stressful (Figley, 1982, 1983), and recovery can take years. The emotional attachments of family and friendship enable us to feel safe, secure, and loved (Figley, 1973; McCubbin & Figley, 1983a). The recent experience of a large group of Americans held hostage in Iran provides an illustration of this phenomenon (Figley, 1980;

Figley & McCubbin, 1983): the hostages' families at home experienced more stress than many of the hostages. For example, while the daily routine of the hostages was highly regimented and predictable, with little access to new information, the hostages' families were constantly bombarded with new information about the captivity experience (most often false rumors), and their routine constantly changed. Frequently, families of hostages were forced to respond to a wide variety of new situations they neither welcomed nor were prepared to deal with.

Chiasmal Effect: "Infecting" the Family with Trauma. In the process of attending to the victimization of a family member, supportive family members themselves are touched emotionally, albeit indirectly. They are affected by the reactions of the victimized family member through their efforts to help. Figley (1983) has described this phenomenon as secondary catastrophic stress response. Others have used other terms to describe this and similar responses.

A recent study by Kishur and Figley (1987) has presented evidence of this phenomenon long observed in the clinical literature. They describe the phenomenon of the "transmission" of behaviors in general and emotional experiences in particular as the chiasmal effects of traumatic stressors. Specifically, they define it as "the phenomenon of behaviors, impressions, actions, attitudes, or emotions which are first seen in one person following an emotionally traumatic event and subsequently observed in a supporter at a later time" (p. 3).

In their study of crime victims and their supporters—especially family members—Kishur and Figley (1987) note that "as expected, the major predictor of *supporter distress was victim distress* [and] it is clear that a pattern of effects emerged in both the victim and supporter. The crime victims as well as their supporters suffered from the crime episode long after the initial crisis had passed. Symptoms of depression, social isolation, disruptions of daily routine, and suspicious feelings of persecution affected the lives of these persons" (p. 18).

Thus, in the process of abating post-traumatic stress reactions, supporters are quite susceptible to being traumatized themselves. It is especially important, therefore, that *each person who appears to be suffering from post-traumatic stress reactions be viewed within a family context* of those victimized indirectly as a result of their concern for the victim.

As researchers—and as human beings—we clinicians often attend too much to those directly exposed to traumatic events. Those who care about these "victims" are rarely acknowledged as also being victims, as suffering from the same extraordinary stressors and as struggling to put their lives back together.

My approach to treating traumatized families recognizes these struggles. In my work with families I try to assist each member to face and eliminate any unwanted consequences of stressors and to do it with minimal cost to other family members.

Yet there are some traumatic events or situations that are particularly difficult to prevent and treat. This is certainly true for intrafamily trauma.

Intrafamily Trauma. Families certainly have the capacity to be extremely helpful in enabling family members in *recovering* from traumatic stressors. They may become traumatized through their assistance. They may also be traumatized from the abuse of other family members.

It is well established in the research and treatment literature that families can be the *context for victimization.* According to the U.S. Department of Justice, Federal Bureau of Investigation (1986), the highest incidence of homicide is in families and between lovers. Family violence and abuse have probably always been a major health problem, and public awareness of this problem in the past two decades has led to major legislation and policies for protection from this form of abuse. Families traumatized from intrafamily abuse are often the most difficult to detect and treat. This is due primarily to the difficulty in establishing mutual trust, commitment, and supportiveness between the victim(s) and victimizer(s). The most effective methods of treatment will be discussed in Chapter Five.

Systemic Traumatic Stress

So how do people respond to these stressors? Before discussing how they respond as a family, I think it is important to discuss individual stress response.

Individual Level. Considerable research and writing exist on the assessment and treatment of *individuals* traumatized by various stressors (for example, war, violent crime, natural disaster, terrorism, family abuse) (see, for example, Figley, 1985c, 1986b). Indeed, the literature of traumatic stress began with the earliest medical writings in 1900 B.C. in the first discussion of what would later be described as hysteria (Veith, 1965). Trimble (1981) has provided an important history of traumatic stress that demonstrates the intense interest in this area, particularly within Western culture from the sixteenth century to the present.

The area of stress and coping seemed to evolve separately from that of traumatic stress, however, with Claude Bernard's (see Selye, 1956) focus on the *milieu interieur,* or internal environment, of a living organism, the importance of which remains fairly constant irrespective of its external environment. Walter B. Cannon (1939) built on this concept of "homeostasis," the ability of the body to remain in a constant state, providing staying power. This is roughly equivalent to a heating system within a building regulated in part by a thermostat.

My work in the area of human stress and coping emerged in the mid 1970s with a concern about Vietnam veterans and their families (Figley, 1975a, 1975b, 1975c, 1976a, 1976b, 1978). I have always found the earliest conceptualization about stress suggested by Hans Selye (1956) to be particularly useful. He defined stress as the "state manifested by a specific syndrome which consists of all the nonspecifically-induced changes within a biologic system" (p. 64). Later he defined stress more simply: "The nonspecific response of the body to any demand made upon it" (1974, p. 14). Equally important, he was the first to suggest that stress is not simply nervous tension or even exclusively distressing, that stress is something to be avoided but that complete freedom from stress is death.

Even more helpful is Selye's discovery of the biological stress syndrome, or general adaptation syndrome (GAS), which describes the body's general method of coping with any type of stressor. Briefly, the syndrome includes three phases. The *alarm* reaction involves the body's initially reacting to a stressor; its resistance is reduced, and with a particularly overwhelming and powerful stress death may occur. But most often the body adjusts and, through the *resistance* phase, draws on its energy reserves to cope with the stressor. All indicators of stress exhibited in the alarm phase have disappeared. However, with repeated exposure to a stressor, the body enters the final phase, *exhaustion.* Here the body exhausts its adaptive energy; the signs of the alarm phase reappear, but now they are irreversible, and unless something is done quickly death may occur. This model partially explains what appears to be a "delayed" stress reaction in both individuals and systems. In reality, the sudden occurrence of the stress reactions was actually a reoccurrence, damped temporarily by efforts to resist the stressor.

Today, traumatic stress is recognized as a separate field within the social sciences (see, for example, Figley, 1988c), complete with a set of concepts to help identify and clarify the most important factors for understanding and treating traumatized families. Yet little attention has focused on the impact of social relationships of these individuals, especially how the social system or family changes.

Among the first efforts to recognize the role of social relationships in traumatic stress was Hill's (1949) classical study of the families of World War II veterans. Most observers consider Hill to have originated the concept of family stress. He was the first to suggest that the system of the family is greatly affected by crisis events such as war and postwar reunion. This sociological orientation emerged into what was later to be called the ABCX model of family crisis (Hill, 1949; Hill & Hansen, 1965) and has evolved into the current Double ABCX model (McCubbin et al., 1980) and subsequent models (see, for example, McCubbin & Patterson, 1983; Montgomery, 1982).

Model of Family Adaptation to Trauma. Our best guess about the *process* by which families adapt to highly stressful, traumatizing events is illustrated in Figure 1. This model or diagram builds on the important work of Hill, Hansen, McCubbin, Patterson, and others referenced above. Different than earlier models, however, we view the adaptation to trauma process in more *systemic* terms. Specifically, we believe that adaptation is a continual process that can either help or hinder current and future family functioning but most often does both.

The stressor (S_1) is defined as an *event or series of events that demands immediate attention to control.* This might be a house fire or natural disaster and may or may not cause a crisis or traumatize the family. Whether trauma occurs depends on the two major categories of factors: the resources of the family (R_1) and the perceptions (P_1) about the stressors held by family members, particularly those in the most powerful and influential positions within the family. We define pretrauma family resources as *those tangible* (for example, material, economic) *and intangible* (for example, effective coping methods, attitudes, cohesiveness, cooperativeness) *factors that are useful in solving problems.*

We define pretrauma family perceptions as *the collective set of beliefs about the stressors that, in turn, may or may not make it traumatizing for the system.*

A family traumatic event is defined as *an event in which there is a general sense that the family is in some kind of danger or major upheaval that involves all or one of its members.*

Getting back to the model, at this point the family begins to deal with the trauma, crisis, or emergency as best they can. The stressors with the trauma (for example, living in temporary housing for families who have suffered the loss of their home) may be limited to a few or may be a large number of post-traumatic stressors (S_n).

We define these post-traumatic stressors as the *accumulation of stressors and strains placed on the family system during and following the traumatic event.* These stressors can include the stressor event and its associated hardships, normative transitions, prior unresolved strains, consequences of the family's efforts to cope, and intrafamily and social ambiguity.

Similar to factors in the pretrauma period, adaptation to

Figure 1. Systemic Adaptation-to-Trauma Process.

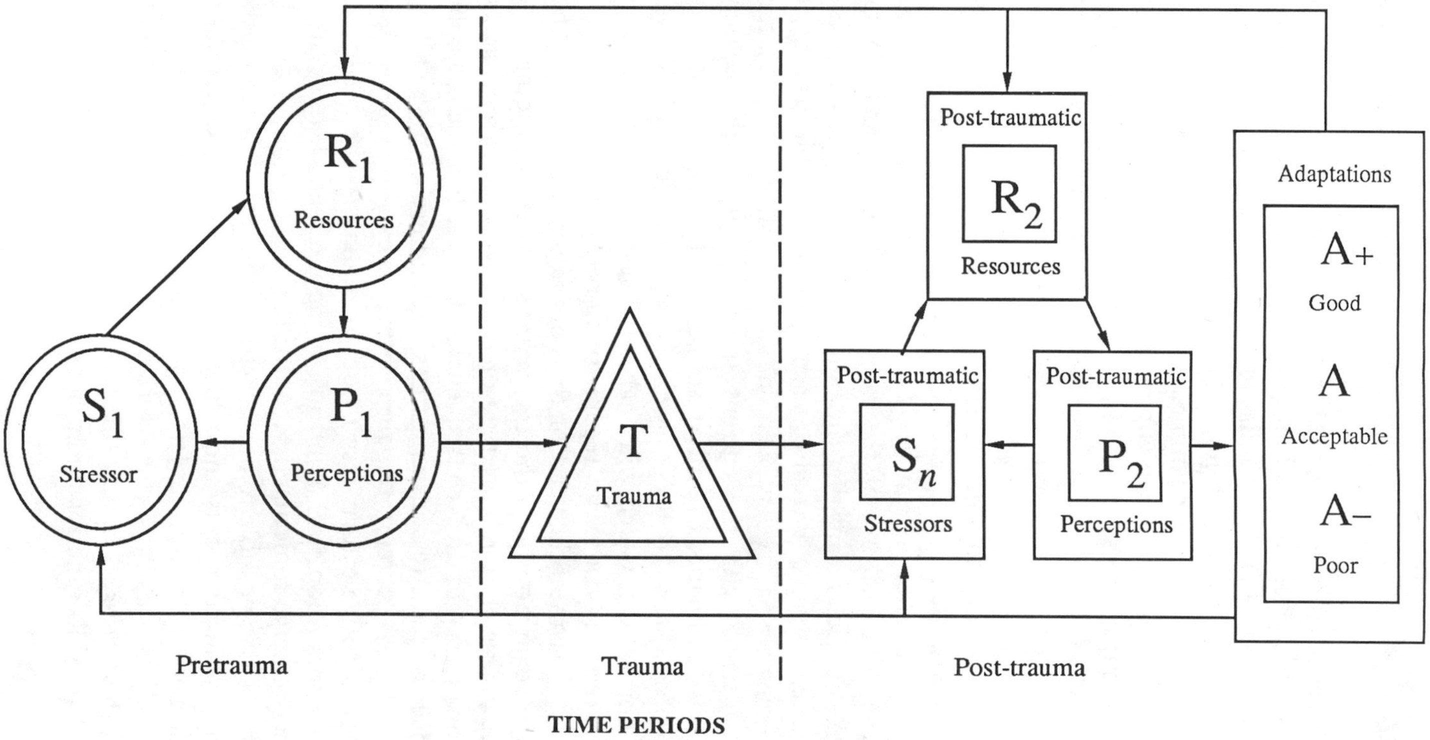

TIME PERIODS

Pretrauma   Trauma   Post-trauma

these stressors is a function of two major categories of factors: resources utilized to adopt (R_2) and the evolving perceptions of the family (P_2). Also similar to the pretrauma period, these concepts are defined as follows. Post-traumatic family resources are *those tangible* (for example, material, economic) *and intangible* (for example, effective coping methods, attitudes, cohesiveness, cooperativeness) *factors that are useful in recovering from the crisis and aftermath of the traumatic events.* Post-traumatic family perceptions are defined as *the collective set of beliefs about the stressors that, in turn, lead to the development and maintenance of an adaptation to the traumatic event and subsequent stressors.*

Adaptation can be reached at any one of a number of levels. At one end of the range is extremely good adaptation (A+), which means that the family not only coped well with the current trauma but also learned some valuable lessons; their coping repertoire has been enhanced in recovering even further in dealing with the current trauma. This positive adaptation leads to enhanced family resources during the current recovery process (loop to R_2) as well as in the basic family resources (loop to R_1), which will enable the system to both prevent and successfully cope with future stressors (loop to R_2).

At the other end of the continuum, however, the family can adapt poorly to the traumatic situation. By doing so, they may have chosen a strategy or tactic with short-term gains but long-term negative consequences. Use of drugs and alcohol to manage the stressful symptoms and the use of physical or psychological coercion to gain control are examples. These ineffective adaptive efforts result both in adding to the current list of stressors (loop to S_n) and in sowing the seeds for stressors that may emerge sometime in the future (loop to S_1).

Is it possible to detect which families will be strengthened by traumatic events and which will not? Research from several decades by many scholars appears to indicate a dozen or so factors that tend to characterize families who adapt poorly to highly stressful events (dysfunctional families) and those who adapt well (functional families).

Functional Family Coping

McCubbin and Figley (1983a) and Figley (1983) identify eleven characteristics that tend to differentiate families who cope well with stress from those who do not. These characteristics are applicable to families struggling with the stress associated with highly stressful events. They include (1) clear acceptance of the stressor, (2) family-centered locus of the problem, (3) solution-oriented problem solving, (4) high tolerance, (5) clear and direct expressions of commitment and affections, (6) open and effective communication utilization, (7) high family cohesion, (8) flexible family roles, (9) efficient resource utilization, (10) absence of violence, and (11) infrequency of substance use. Each will be discussed briefly below in terms of families who cope effectively with stress and either avoid or quickly recover from traumatic experiences.

Clear Acceptance of Stressor. Effective families are able to quickly accept that their family is being forced to struggle with a highly stressful event or series of events. They may find themselves temporarily bewildered by overwhelming events but quickly recover and begin to mobilize their energy and resources for action.

Family-Centered Locus of Problem. Effective families quickly shift the focus of the problem or stressor away from any one family member or set of members and recognize it as a problem or challenge for the entire family. The Murray family, to their credit, quickly recognized that Tammy's depression was part of and, indeed, a result of the pileup of stressors impacting on everyone in the family, and that all of the stressors must be addressed at some point.

Solution-Oriented Problem Solving. Effective families get stuck only briefly on who is to blame for the current crisis or trauma and then move on to mobilize their resources to correct the situation together.

High Tolerance. Effective families' members tend to have even more tolerance for each other during a highly stressful time than in times of relative calm. They tend to recognize the need for conciliation, patience, and consideration in times that require cooperation and teamwork.

Clear and Direct Expressions of Commitment and Affections. Similarly, effective families tend to have members who are especially clear and direct about their feelings toward one another, particularly expressions of commitment to each other—irrespective of whether times are difficult or not. Moreover, effective families are generous with their praise and signs of affection, both verbal and nonverbal.

Open and Effective Communication Utilization. Not only do members of effective families communicate with one another about affection and commitment, but also the quality and quantity of their discussions are higher than those of the average family. They tend to have few sanctions against when and what to talk about and, indeed, enjoy talking with one another about a wide range of topics.

High Family Cohesion. Effective families have members who enjoy each other's company, miss each other when they are away, are proud to be part of the family, and speak with pride about each other. This cohesiveness is especially important when the family is traumatized, since the tendency for most families is to abandon other family members when they may need the family more than ever.

Flexible Family Roles. All family members play many roles within their family: completing household chores, earning and consuming income, communicating with relatives and friends, and other tasks on behalf of the family. In effective families these roles are often played by more than one person. This is especially important in times of crisis and trauma, when one or more members may be unable to function effectively.

Efficient Resource Utilization. Effective families are able to access their own resources (interpersonal, material) and those outside the family—either professional or nonprofessional—without difficulty and with little sense of embarrassment. Indeed, they are able to recognize that under certain circumstances relying on others is especially important, since they would expect to provide similar services to their friends and kin who might be in similar difficult circumstances.

Absence of Violence. Effective families, irrespective of the amount of stress and trauma they must endure, do not resort to violence against themselves or their members. Highly emotional outbursts, from screaming to weeping, are normal and expected, however, in traumatic times in families.

Infrequency of Substance Use. Similarly, though adult family members may drink socially and use prescribed drugs, these are not used as a method of stress reduction. Moreover, irrespective of the cause of addiction, successful families rarely include members who are addicted to substances such as alcohol, narcotics, or even prescription drugs. In functional families, these problems are most often corrected as soon as they are adequately recognized.

Dysfunctional Family Coping

There are, of course, families who utilize dysfunctional coping methods in efforts to avert or ameliorate a traumatic situation. McCubbin and Figley (1983a) and Figley (1983) note eleven characteristics of a dysfunctional or ineffective family. To a certain extent they are the obverse of the functional coping characteristics. They include (1) denial or misperception of the stressor, (2) individual-centered locus of the problem, (3) blame-oriented problem solving, (4) low tolerance, (5) indirect or missing expressions of commitment and affections, (6) closed and ineffective communication utilization, (7) low or poor family cohesion, (8) rigid family roles, (9) inefficient resource utilization, (10) utilization of violence, (11) frequent use of substances.

In Chapter Four we discuss an interview method to effectively assess the extent to which families are successful at coping with stress. This determination is important, of course, in establishing the most appropriate treatment program for client families.

Conclusion

In this chapter I have tried to emphasize that families are a valuable resource for helping members recover from highly stressful traumatic experiences. However, the family system may suffer in the process, depending on the particular resources within the family and the adaptive perceptions that emerge over time. The families most likely to require our services, of course, are those that are the most dysfunctional, have the fewest resources, and hold the most hampered perspectives.

In the next chapter I describe my empowering orientation to helping traumatized families. As I have tried to explain, it is based on the lessons learned by studying *functional* families—those most successful in adapting to trauma and recovering to become even more resilient, even more effective and efficient in dealing with future adversities.

Recognizing the natural capacity of the family system for self-regulation, self-correction, and recovery from catastrophes and less extraordinary stressors, in the next chapter I try to describe my orientation to helping individuals, particularly within the family context. It should be clear then, if it is not clear already, that I am in awe of the family system. Certainly, families are responsible for considerable human misery: incest, physical and psychological abuse, discouragement, depression, loneliness. Yet I have witnessed, as a researcher, as a therapist, and as a family member, quite remarkable growth and healing that takes place within families.

Helping traumatized families involves respecting their capacity to heal themselves and being sure that we promote and not inhibit that natural capacity.

CHAPTER 3

Empowering Families:
A New Approach to Treatment

Over the years, in working with hundreds of mental health professionals, I have tried to convey my feelings and values about helping traumatized people and families, not just my therapeutic methods.

In Chapter One I began to describe how I try to be useful to traumatized families by first discussing why I believe that families, rather than the individual, are the appropriate unit of intervention. Here I will first describe some of the building blocks of my theoretical orientation prior to introducing it. Later I will discuss the major goals of my work, which emerge from my theoretical orientation. The latter part of the chapter will specify my preconditions for helping or treating traumatized families.

Theoretical Orientation Building Blocks

As noted earlier, my empowerment approach to helping traumatized families borrows heavily from crisis intervention theory, traumatic stress studies, cognitive psychology, behavioral therapy, and systems theory. I believe that it would be useful to briefly summarize these theoretical contributions.

Crisis Intervention Theory. Although relatively new as a professional orientation, crisis intervention emerged from a social need that arose when families and communities were no longer reliable as a resource for helping people and families in emergencies. There are certainly many crisis intervention theorists who have made extremely important contributions. My own theories of change have been most influenced by Lindemann (1944), Caplan (1964), and most recently by Jacobson, Strickler, and Morley (1968). I include the contributions of grief work here as well.

Lindemann (1944) discovered the long-term effects of the 1943 Coconut Grove fire in Boston not only among those who survived it directly but also among the families and friends of those who died. He was among the first to demonstrate that there is a set of psychological characteristics common to survivors of a wide variety of crises. Though we can quibble about the precision of his classifications, he was among the first to suggest that survivors pass through various stages in the process of working through their traumatic experiences.

Caplan (1964, 1974) demonstrated that the crisis survivor attempts to maintain a homeostatic balance with her or his environment. When the survivor's homeostasis is threatened, perhaps by a traumatic stressor, the survivor attempts to engage in problem-solving activity to restore the previous condition. Otherwise, the survivor becomes confused and disoriented both intrapsychically and interpersonally.

Jacobson, Strickler, and Morley (1968) have contributed two use models, generic and individual, which attempt to clarify for the crisis intervention practitioner what she or he should look for in the survivor client and suggest when and how to be most helpful. The generic model describes the predictable or identifiable stress reactions and coping methods of crisis survivors. This model accounts for the general process of recovery. In contrast, the individual model of crisis recovery focuses on personal and environmental factors, the how and why of the crisis.

Finally, my empowerment approach to helping traumatized families is indebted to the general field of death and dying, also called "grief work" or "bereavement theory." The work of Bowlby (1961, 1969, 1980), Parks (1964, 1972), and Raphael (1973, 1983) has suggested but not identified the direct link between traumatic stress and grief reactions and their subsequent treatments.

Traumatic Stress Studies. More than any other area, traumatic stress studies have shaped my thinking about human systems reactions to extraordinary stress. Perhaps this is because I have been among the primary contributors to this area (see, for example, Figley, 1978, 1985c, 1986b). As noted earlier, the study of the symptoms of traumatic stress, particularly those associated with hysteria, dates to one of the world's first medical textbooks. Elsewhere I have discussed the history, theory, assessment, treatment, and research initiatives in this new field of study (Figley, 1988b).

Cognitive and Behavioral Psychology. As a psychologist and human development specialist, my primary intellectual orientation has been cognitive and behavioral psychology. The basic propositions and assumptions in these areas shape or at least influence my conceptualization, methods of study, and treatment of traumatized families. Certainly the two-factor learning theory suggested by Mowrer (1947, 1960), emerging from both classical Pavlovian conditioning and instrumental learning, is an important basic framework for my work. Moreover, the experiments of Solomon and his associates (Solomon, Kamin, & Wynne, 1953; Solomon & Wynne, 1954) with aversive stimuli were the first to link experimentally induced avoidance behavior and phobia. Finally, the more recent empirically derived propositions associated with the link between stress reduction and exposure to conditioned stimuli in the absence of an unconditioned stimulus (Mineka, 1979), implosion therapy, and systematic desensitization (Rimm & Masters, 1979; Kazdin & Wilcoxin, 1976; Levis & Hare, 1977) have been influential to my work.

Systems Theory. Systems theory has emerged as the primary theoretical orientation for family therapists worldwide (see Haley, 1984). As noted in Chapter One, by viewing the family as a system and individual members and their dyadic and triadic relationships within the family as subsystems, psychotherapists develop intervention programs to ameliorate various presenting problems of both the individual and the family.

Systems theorists most influential to my work are those who have attempted to conceptualize a diagnostic categorization for families and those who have adopted either a psycho-educational or a strategic approach to treating family systems.

Olson and his associates (Olson, Sprenkle, & Russell, 1979; Russell & Olson, 1983; Olson, Russell, & Sprenkle, 1989) provide an extremely useful diagnostic methodology for families with their circumplex model of marital systems. They utilize *adaptability* and *cohesion* as the key concepts in measuring and diagnosing family pathology. The circumplex model is among the most empirically grounded systems approaches. It is designed to both generate information about particular families and organize that information into relevant treatment goals.

The strategic systemic treatment approaches of Haley (1973, 1976, 1984), Madanes (1984), the Mental Research Institute group (Watzlawick, Beavin, & Jackson, 1967; Watzlawick, Weakland, & Fisch, 1974; Fisch, Weakland, & Segal, 1982), and most recently Fraser (1989) offer extremely innovative methods for viewing and changing family systems and subsystems.

General Approach to Treatment/Intervention

My approach could be characterized as both a prevention and an empowering, trauma-focused family therapy. I attempt to *empower the family to make peace with the past* and take charge of their lives. It is a prevention orientation in that I attempt to mitigate the presenting stress and enable the family to avoid any unwanted future stress.

Whereas *primary prevention* mental health approaches (see, for example, Guerney, Guerney, & Cooney, 1985) focus on helping clients to *avoid dysfunction*, secondary prevention focuses on helping clients to *avoid further dysfunction.* Similarly, in my empowering approach I work with those families who are at risk of developing chronic stress-related problems (for example, PTSD). I not only attempt to help traumatized families stabilize their current situation; through a standard psychoeducational approach, I also help them develop or supplement basic family relations skills to foster social supportiveness.

Although family psychotherapy or family therapy dates

back to the 1950s, applications to traumatic stress did not emerge until the mid 1970s (Figley, 1976a, 1976b). Research has suggested that those individuals most traumatized by their experiences are the most impaired interpersonally (Figley, 1985b; Green, Wilson, & Lindy, 1985), that traumatic residue eventually becomes enmeshed in the victim's interpersonal network (Figley, 1983), and that there is a clear need for marriage and family therapy to both improve the support and promote recovery of the network (family) itself (Figley, 1983).

Duke Stanton and I (Stanton & Figley, 1978) explicated in detail the suggested method of intervention in family systems suffering from PTSD. We indicated that the therapist has two major and overlapping tasks: (1) to assess the degree of severity of the member's disorder, particularly how the family tends to modulate it through its specific relationship dysfunctions; and (2) to develop and implement an intervention program to deal with both the stress disorder and the associated dysfunctions within the system. In addition to my orientation as a behavioral scientist, at that time my approach drew primarily from systems theory and the emerging field of traumatic stress. Although the basic principles for helping traumatized families have been in the literature since 1978 (Figley, 1983, 1986a, 1986c; Figley & Sprenkle, 1978; Stanton & Figley, 1978), few specific procedures have been described in any detail.

Making Peace with the Past. Today, my focus is on understanding and utilizing the family system and the family's natural effort to recover from traumatic events. I attempt to help the family recapitulate the most important factors associated with these events and learn to manage the memories of these events more effectively and satisfactorily. By doing so, they not only effectively cope with the traumatic and post-traumatic stress but also are able to make peace with the past and are more prepared to face current and future challenges.

Psychoeducation. Finally, I am concerned with equipping the family with the necessary knowledge about the traumatic stress recovery process. I assign them things to read and equip them to explain trauma and traumatic stress to children in the family. In addition, I believe that it is important to help families develop effective systemic or family resources, such as communication, problem-solving, and conflict resolution skills, to enable them to avoid stressful events in the future.

Family Social Supportiveness. I am concerned with equipping the family with the systemic resources not only to speed their recovery to the current trauma but also to help them avoid future ones or to recover more quickly. This is done by developing more social supportiveness within the family through the development of family relations skills.

As noted earlier, social support is a critical resource for human survival. This support can take many forms: love, affection, kindness, companionship, a sense of belonging, protection, advice, favors, encouragement. Social support is now viewed in the social sciences as one of the most important of human resources (Pilisuk & Parks, 1986; Gottlieb, 1983, 1988; Brownell & Shumaker, 1984; Shumaker & Brownell, 1985). Because it is a critical factor in coping with traumatic stress, we attempt to foster and develop this resource. As noted earlier, in addition to *treating* or helping the family to ameliorate the unwanted consequences of traumatic events and memories, we want to *prevent* further deterioration of the family system. At the same time we want to help in *preventing future traumatic stress reactions* from past and future traumas.

Many other factors often difficult to define and measure are the products of friendship and family relations. There is considerable variation in the quality of social support in all types of systems (for example, work units, clubs, teams). This is certainly the case in families.

I strive to assess the degree to which family members are currently supportive to one another, the degree to which they really *want* to be supportive, and the degree to which they are *capable* of being supportive. Through modeling and training in some basic family relations skills, social supportiveness can be increased significantly.

Family Relations Skills. A major element of treating families, particularly families in crisis, is focusing on the development of a variety of interpersonal relationship skills. These include behaviors that appear to lead to effective and efficient (1) exchange of information between family members, (2) problem solving, and (3) conflict resolution.

By fostering family relations skills, family members are able to fully exploit their own individual resources and those of other family members in helping to seek and resolve the current crisis. There is a wide variety of models for teaching these skills to people within a family context. An excellent example is Guerney's (1977) relationship enhancement (RE) program. Developing interpersonal relationship skills will also be discussed more fully later in this book when the treatment approach is discussed.

Treatment Preconditions

With some sense of what is involved in my empowerment approach to treating traumatized families, I would like to briefly discuss what I consider to be the important treatment preconditions to designing a treatment program for any particular traumatized family. First, it is important to screen families carefully to determine if they are suited for this kind of therapy. The following questions should be answered, if at all possible: (1) What set of circumstances brought this family to treatment? (2) How committed are they as a family? (3) Is psychological or systemic trauma a critical issue in this family? (4) How much are family members suffering? (5) Can some method of family relations skills training be developed?

What Set of Circumstances Brought This Family to Treatment? Some families seek assistance because they are certain that their difficulties are related to a traumatic event. Others do not link their current difficulties to past traumas. The Murray family is an example of this. They sought assistance out of concern for their daughter. Shortly after gathering background information, however, it quickly became apparent that the family system was struggling to cope with the consequences of past events.

Also, it is important to determine how long the family has endured the traumatic stress. Was it recent, such as the sudden death of a family member? Has it been an ongoing problem that has only now become a crisis?

The circumstances of presenting problems and chronicity are important to planning and beginning the therapy program, since the family must believe that their current difficulties are at least in part linked with traumatic events. This will enable the therapist to proceed quickly once the treatment program begins.

How Committed Are They as a Family? Appreciating that the family is struggling with traumatic stress is only one part of the task for the therapist at this point, however. Some families seek professional assistance to have "something fixed" and not to be fixed themselves. For example, parents are more likely to commit to a therapy program that, they are assured, will result in the child's conforming to their wishes than to a program that forces the parents to change.

Thus, commitment to treatment may be quite high under some circumstances, such as making the youngest child mind his parents. Commitment may be low if the treatment requires the parents to change their parenting methods.

A family therapist I was supervising treated a family who was court-ordered to seek therapy for their six-year-old son, who had been caught sexually molesting a neighbor's toddler. It was clear that the family only wanted to have the six-year-old treated and that they felt their presence was only to reinforce and "witness" the treatment. It quickly became obvious to the therapist and to the family that the entire family had been traumatized by the event, and they were suffering from shame, anger, and confusion. In a short time the focus of the therapy expanded from the son to his family and eventually to the family of the toddler.

Moreover, clients who have been traumatized not only often deny the long-term negative consequences of the traumatic events but also are often concerned about recapitulating these painful memories. As one forty-year-old father once explained to me: "Doc, how will I know that what I uncover and let out of the bag won't turn on me and I won't be able to get it back into the bag?" The critical issue is not that families are unwilling to guarantee that they will recapitulate the past but that they trust the therapist enough to risk such options sometime in the future.

Traumatized families may lack commitment to treatment, then, if it involves dealing with painful memories of the past. Later I will discuss and provide illustrations of waning levels of client commitment. It is important in the beginning, however, that therapy not start until and unless clients understand the objectives and course of therapy and are fully committed. At times of uncertainty it is necessary for the therapist and clients to strike a deal that the clients commit to at least a brief trial period of several sessions (say, two to five). At the end of this period the scope and progress of therapy are evaluated.

It is important, irrespective of the means by which it is established, that the entire family be committed to the treatment program. In effect, all members need to be committed and willing to at least *consider* changing their own behavior and relationships with other family members.

Is Psychological or Systemic Trauma a Critical Issue in This Family? Obviously it is important to establish the fact that we are working with a traumatized family. It is not necessary that *anyone* in the family have a diagnosable case of PTSD to qualify as a "traumatized family."

As I tried to explain in Chapter One, traumatized families are those who are attempting to cope with an extraordinary stressor. This stressor or set of stressors has disrupted their lives, their routine, sense of well-being, and confidence in the safety and predictability of daily life.

In the next chapter I will describe what I believe should be the established criteria for PTSD in systems. (*Note:* The American Association for Marriage and Family Therapy will soon propose an equivalent of DSM-III applied to families as opposed to individuals.) Briefly, the following criteria apply: evidence of at least one highly stressful event experienced by at least one family member and indirectly by at least one other.

How Much Are Family Members Suffering? In working with traumatized families over the years, I have come to appreciate the fact that some families suffer more than others, though both families were exposed to the same stressors and show clear signs of being traumatized. Similarly, I have served as a mental health consultant on numerous major catastrophes. Only a small percentage of victims and victimized families avail themselves of professional mental health services, and only a slightly larger percentage actually need these services. The others are not "suffering" enough. They are able to draw on their own resources and those of their social support networks to carry them through their ordeal.

Even before any assessments are made, an observant therapist should be able to detect clear evidence of hardship. In the best of cases there are general fear, anxiety, and concern about the long-term effects of traumatic events and the prognosis for recovery. In the worst cases, of course, the family is demoralized, helpless, and not working together. Indeed, in many worst cases there are physical violence, substance abuse, and other reactions that may be associated with coping with the ordeal.

I have found that it is critical to clearly identify, document, and seek consensus from the family about these unwanted consequences and suffering and make them a part of the objectives of the treatment program.

Can Some Method of Family Relations Skills Training Be Developed? This may seem more like an early treatment objective than a precondition. I see it more as the latter because some client families are unwilling or unable to develop such skills. This may be due to one or more members' "not believing in such nonsense."

In treating PTSD in individuals, I make certain that there is some method of stress reduction/relaxation that is utilized by the client. This allows the client to control her or his stress reactions—both in and out of the therapy session—enables the client to gain a sense of mastery and competence over the often feared symptoms of stress reactions, and enables the client to prevent or control the stress reactions associated with future traumatic events or simple stressors.

Isomorphic to my methods of treating individuals suffering from traumatic stress, I believe that helping families recover from trauma requires the utilization (or establishment) of family relations skills. As noted elsewhere, this includes but is not limited to skills that are linked to social supportiveness: communication skills, empathy, conflict resolution, problem solving, negotiation, and other observable, measurable behaviors linked empirically to effective family relationships. I once agreed to see a family who was experiencing a crisis. The father had recently been suspended from the police force of a large city because of his abuse of alcohol. He was receiving treatment for this problem, yet his family was experiencing considerable stress, partly due to his substance abuse but mostly due to the pileup of stressors over the last year or so.

After the first session I discovered that neither the father nor the eldest child (fourteen-year-old son) was willing to develop what they described as "touchy feely skills" for the sake of the treatment program. Rather, they wanted me to listen to them and come up with some solution that would "fix" the problems they were experiencing.

If the initial assessments establish that some or all family members need at least a minimal level of these skills, a method of skills training needs to be established. Several of these methods of family enrichment or skills training will be discussed in the coming chapters. What is important at this point in the treatment program is to determine the most appropriate program of training if interpersonal skills are indeed lacking.

In the case of the family of the substance-abusing father, they later agreed to my requirements. They recognized that in order for them to take an active role in solving their traumatic stress and preventing and more quickly coping with future ones, it was critical that they develop some additional skills.

Briefly, my approach to helping traumatized families emerges from my theoretical orientation to viewing and treating dysfunctional families, tempered by my genuine respect for the natural resourcefulness of families. I try to *empower* the family by creating the kind of intervention context that results in the resolution of the traumatizing experience but, just as importantly, that results in the family's giving themselves most of the credit for the accomplishment. Moreover, this approach makes the family feel more confident to face any future traumatic experiences equipped with the necessary information, skills, and problem-solving methods.

In subsequent chapters I try to describe in sufficient detail the steps I take in assessing and helping traumatized families. In the next chapter I begin to present my approach to psychometrics and diagnosis.

CHAPTER 4

Assessing the Family's Level of Stress

Traumatized families, as noted in Chapter Two, are sometimes difficult to detect if they do not represent themselves as being traumatized. Some families, of course, recognize the need to work through some particular catastrophe in their life: the death of a family member, some violent victimization, or other circumstances.

Most often, however, families begin to seek help by presenting a problem different than the traumatic event. Through the course of intervention it becomes apparent that the family is traumatized. These families are very difficult to spot, since traumatized families often can function quite well for long periods of time.

The Murray family is an example of a family that appeared to be concerned only with helping the daughter avoid suicidal behavior. However, just under the surface they were struggling with the aftermath of events that began long before the daughter was born.

Conversely, some families endure highly stressful events and show no lasting unwanted effects. It is unwise when helping these families to linger long on such events other than to recognize the family's strength and coping ability. Detecting which family is traumatized and recovering normally and which is recovering poorly is a challenge.

Helping the traumatized family and other traumatized systems requires some careful documentation. This includes not only each family member's symptoms and perspectives but also the collective, systemic factors as well. In this chapter I will discuss the various methods for assessing individual and family trauma. I will begin with a description of the clinical interview protocol I follow. It includes a series of interrelated questions. The answers to these questions provide insight not only into how each family member has engaged the trauma but also into the system engagement of the *family as a system of interacting and interdependent members.*

Clinical Interview

I have found that during the initial interview with a traumatized family and, perhaps, in one or more subsequent sessions, certain information is very important. Sometimes I collect this information with the entire family present. Most often, however, I get it from whoever is willing to tell me and under whatever circumstances. Most often I first talk with either the identified client/patient or, in the case of a child, her or his parents. Sometime early in the case, however, I need to ascertain, among other things, to what extent the family has coped with the traumatic event and its aftermath. Often the methods families select in coping with a highly stressful event or series of events may be as upsetting and stressful as the initial traumatic stressors.

In Chapter Two the typical coping characteristics that distinguish between functional and dysfunctional family coping were identified. I have found that it is useful in the initial interview to identify the characteristic ways my client family copes with crisis. Following are some questions that address each of the major family coping characteristics. The information such questions produce will be useful in developing the specific ways in which I try to help the traumatized family.

Do Family Members Have a Clear Understanding and Acceptance of the Sources of Stress Affecting Them? Traumatized families are easier to help if they can identify cause-effect or the stressor-stress reaction paradigms that apply to their circumstances. In contrast, client families who are confused about how or why they are dysfunctional or who have major differences in beliefs or perceptions among family members—particularly between parents and children or husbands and wives—are more difficult to treat. Some families simply have had no opportunity to focus on their circumstances and may thus require some time and discussion to adequately address this question.

Do Family Members See the Difficulties They Face to Be Family Centered, or Do They Blame One or Two Family Members? I can often predict in the initial interview which client family will cope well with adversity and will require only a few sessions of my help. These are families who will move (or have already moved) quickly from blaming or finding fault with a family member to recognition that everyone in the family shares both the blame and the credit for their current predicament. This is particularly true for the parents' assumption of responsibility. These families appear to pull together emotionally and recognize that irrespective of what caused the problems they face, the family faces them together, that the entire family is being affected by this crisis, and that it will require everyone's cooperation to solve the problem. Indeed, many of these families tend to be better off as a result of their struggles, which I will discuss later.

Do Family Members Appear to Be Solution Oriented or Blame Oriented? Similarly, I have found that there is a good prognosis for families who tend to be anxious to move toward solving a problem and whose members avoid blaming each other. This does not mean that these families do not spend sufficient time tracking the causes of their difficulties. It is unwise to move too quickly to solve a problem when there is uncertainty about exactly what constitutes the problem. However, members of families who tend to maintain long-felt resentments, lack trust in one another, and feel discouraged in life tend to blame other family members for past and present circumstances. These families will require considerable attention and patience in working through their traumatic experiences and shifting their patterns of family relationships to more productive methods.

What Are the General Levels of Tolerance for One Another in This Family? Is the family more or less tolerant in times of crisis? Families who cope best become more tolerant and tend to overlook minor violations of social or family rules. Families who cope poorly with stress tend to be even less tolerant than usual in stressful situations, particularly crisis situations. It is as if they adopt a philosophy of "every man for himself" during these times, during which there are few indications that family members look out for each other's welfare.

How Committed Are Family Members to One Another? Similarly, I try to detect the extent to which family members are committed to one another: for protection, emotional comfort, and companionship. Hardy families tend to praise each other, celebrate their victories, and collectively grieve over disappointments.

How Much Affection Is There in This Family? Relatedly, hardy families appear, in both words and actions, to be genuinely affectionate toward one another. Some families rarely demonstrate this affection; there is an absence of kissing, hugging, and even touching. Yet the affection among members is demonstrated by frequent smiles, friendly banter, and general attentiveness. This is in contrast with troubled families who appear ill at ease not only with the therapist but also with each other.

What Are the Quality and Quantity of Communication Among Members in This Family? Hundreds of books are filled with discussions about interpersonal and family communication. Moreover, more than a dozen measures are available that purport to quantify these factors. Later I will describe two measures that I use that do just that. But careful observation of the family during the session will reveal an enormous amount of information.

We family therapists find that observing families interacting reveals a great deal about many characteristics of the system. For the traumatized family, good communication among family members is critical to recovery (see, for example, Figley, 1983, 1985c). A family that fits the following description tends to have reasonably good quality and quantity of family communications: Anyone may talk about anything at any time as long as it was done with at least a minimum amount of courtesy. Moreover, it appears that messages sent are received and acknowledged as they were meant. There is little serious quibbling over semantics. Adequate display of and commitment to understanding and empathy toward one another are apparent.

These signs, of course, are just that—brief indicators. If you are uncertain about interpersonal and family communication, you would benefit from a quick review of the literature in this area.

How Cohesive Is This Family as a Group? Cohesion is an extremely important factor in understanding and helping traumatized families. Olson and his associates, as noted in Chapter Three, view cohesion and adaptability as the key factors in diagnosing family pathology. Do family members like to be with each other as much as they would if they were not in the same family? This is a question I ask myself when I first meet a family. I get a sense of how well they work and cooperate with one another. Functional, hardy, effective families tend to enjoy each other's company, though they may wish to not be together all the time when they have an opportunity. This is particularly true for teens.

How Flexible Are Family Roles? Families today have much more flexible family roles than did earlier generations. This is partly because more women work outside the home, forcing husbands and children to do more at home today than in the past. But there tends to be a wide variation among today's families regarding who performs what family role beyond simply cooking, cleaning, and repairing things. This includes such roles as shopping for the family's food, clothes, household appliances, and furniture; communicating for the family by letter, card, or telephone; protecting the family against intruders, fire, or bad weather; and so on. What is critical in families experiencing a crisis is not who performs these tasks but the extent to which they are shared among at least two family members. It is critical because these families may have members who are unable, from time to time, to perform their duties. Hardy or effective families are able to rely on another family member to perform these vital family functions.

Do Family Members Tend to Utilize or Avoid Resources Outside the Family? It is rather odd that families that most need outside resources such as family therapy are often the most resistant in seeking them. I have found that knowing about the family's history of resource utilization is helpful in planning treatment. For example, various support groups, continuing education classes, skills training, and other supplemental interventions would be very useful to traumatized families in augmenting therapy. Yet some families are very reluctant to utilize these resources, which should thus be incorporated in the services I provide rather than provided by referral.

Do Family Members Serve as a Resource to Others as Well? I have found that families who frequently provide resources to others, such as donations to charities, performing services through places of worship or service clubs (for example, Lions Club or Girl Scouts), or various acts of kindness such as donating a meal to a grieving family tend to be families who are more open to help from others. Moreover, being in a helping role provides the experience of what it is like to be in the position of a therapist. I often draw parallels with the family's own experiences with helping others to my efforts to help them help themselves.

Is There Evidence of Family Violence? Sometimes traumatized families, overwhelmed with emotion and stress, resort to displays of aggressive behavior. For some families, physical violence may have emerged as a coping method, albeit a poor one, to solve problems or at least change the victim's behavior. The use of physical violence may be an isolated incident or may be a part of the pattern of behavior between a parent and children, between husband and wife, or among siblings. Rarely are families satisfied with such patterns, but they tend to become stuck with them. I have found that it is very important to specifically ask about the use of violence. Are there any household rules? What are the consequences if violence does occur? If there is evidence of violence in the family I quickly seek and secure a commitment to substitute other methods for these abusive ones.

Moreover, as soon as possible, I meet with the victim or victims. I do this without calling attention to the abuse in order to not put the victim at greater risk. In the interview I make certain that she or he is not in any danger and determine if the abuse has been or should be reported and if it is wise to proceed.

Sometimes it is clear that the abuse is much more important to the family than the "presenting" trauma. Irrespective of which trauma is the initial focus, I always attempt to address all traumatic stressors generally in the order that the family can deal with them. Most often this means easiest and most recent first, assuming that the family's skill and knowledge about coping are cumulative.

Is There Evidence of Substance Abuse in the Family? Similarly, various forms of substance use and abuse may be part of the traumatized family's difficulties and may have started as a method of coping long before the traumatic event. I have found that any addiction problems will become especially evident during the family's efforts to recover from traumatic stress. Sometimes it may be necessary to address the addiction problem before an effective program for treating the trauma can begin—for example, when the addicted person is unable to stay "straight" during the session. Is this an attempt to disrupt the treatment program? As with individual treatment, I believe that addiction problems must be dealt with first, since they are often easily identified, prior to addressing the traumatic and post-traumatic stress.

This series of questions, then, will provide the therapist with a useful set of knowledge about the capacity of the client family to cope with highly stressful situations. This knowledge will be critical not only in planning the treatment program but also in utilizing some of the information when the program is implemented.

What is most important in this interview is to determine if the family is traumatized and, if so, what resources they have and to what extent intervention is necessary and sufficient. Some families only need reassurance: someone who can explain to them how traumatic stress evolves and is managed and how the family is progressing normally in that process. They will remember your reassuring comments and your invitation to call or come in anytime to help in the healing process. Other families will deny that the traumatic event has much of an influence on them.

The interview is simply an opportunity to gather qualitative, intuition-driven information on the client family and to permit them to become acquainted with you, the therapist and human being.

Measuring Traumatic Stress

In addition to the clinical interview, a good intake session will include a psychometric assessment of the family's traumatic stress and the resources available to cope with these stressors. Those I use regularly are my Traumagram Questionnaire, the Purdue PTSD Scale, the Brief Symptom Inventory (BSI), the Purdue Social Support Scale, and the Family Adaptability and Cohesion Evaluation Scale. All of these measures have been used in research, some quite extensively. These measures should be in addition to any others routinely administered to families.

Traumagram Questionnaire. For many years in working with individual and family clients it became clear that they had experienced more than one single traumatic event. For example, war veterans who had left the military ten to fifteen years earlier had, since the war, experienced a wide variety of catastrophic experiences (for example, auto accidents, sudden unemployment, and other extraordinary cataclysmic events of living).

Moreover, many had been exposed to highly stressful experiences *prior* to military service. That these experiences happened to them was not surprising, and these experiences probably did not occur any more frequently for veterans than for nonveterans.

What is important, however, is that current symptoms of traumatic stress in general and PTSD in particular may be exclusively associated with one event but may also be associated with many. Therefore, to effectively treat traumatic stress, we need to know the true origin or multiple origins of the stress. We may assume, along with the client, that these PTSD symptoms are connected only with the most extraordinary catastrophe, such as the experiences of a war, a violent rape, a terrorist attack, or a hostage taking. Yet with some patience we can detect that the client has experienced (and may still be recovering emotionally from) *several* traumatic events.

With this discovery I have been experimenting with an instrument I call a traumagram (Figley, 1988d). It is somewhat analogous to a genogram since, like a genogram, it guides the therapist to collect specific information that can then be used to chart the traumatic events that have occurred to a person.

Resource A includes the current version of the Traumagram Questionnaire. The client is asked to first identify any traumatic events in her or his life: significant events that were extraordinarily stressful at the time and that left lingering, troubling memories for a time. The rest of the instrument probes for specific dates; names of those also exposed; and a rating of the degree of stressfulness at the time of the event, twelve months later, and at the time of testing. With these data, then, you are able to construct a traumagram, as illustrated in Figure 2.

The Traumagram Questionnaire includes a series of questions that, together, enable the clinician/researcher to develop a profile of both the individual respondent and the social system within which she or he resides. Among other things, the data can be useful in developing a chart. The chart utilizes information about the various distressing events and the period within which the respondent strove to cope with the events. Charting

Figure 2. Example of Traumagram for Fictitious Client.

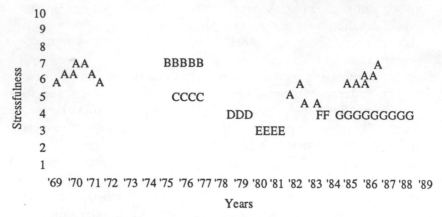

1 = mildly stressful to 10 = unimaginably stressful

Events: A = Vietnam War
        B = bad auto accident
        C = sudden unemployment
        D = child seriously ill
        E = divorce
        F = death of father
        G = cancer

these data in this way results in a diagram that shows the various traumatic experiences and resulting stressors endured by the respondent.

Viewed together, the traumagrams of each member of the family provide a family profile of the tracks of trauma. It enables the clinician to view the current struggles in a broader historical context.

Figure 2 represents Michael Murray's traumatic life experiences. His responses indicated that: (1) seven (A–G) distinct stressors predate the one for which he and his family are seeking treatment; (2) Vietnam War–related stressors were the first catastrophic stressors and lasted from 1969 until 1972, then erupted again at lower levels in 1982 and 1983 and again in 1985 to the time of treatment at higher levels.

The chart not only indicates each major stressor but also shows the multiple and cumulative effects on current functioning.

At the time of treatment Mr. Murray was struggling not only with the memories of war but also with his candor and the potential cumulative effects of an auto accident, sudden unemployment, a child's illness, divorce, and the death of his father.

These data are very useful to us in tracking the individual client's patterns of stress reactions and coping and viewing, together, the family system's reactions and coping.

Traumatic Stress. Measures of traumatic and post-traumatic stress disorders, a rarity only a decade ago, now abound in various forms (Figley, 1988b). These specific measures are being either supplemented or replaced entirely by more generic measures of the stress associated with highly stressful events. These instruments, particularly the more generic, all-purpose ones, are based on various theories of traumatic stress or cognitive appraisal of highly stressful events.

These generic measures tend to be those that focus on either *symptomology,* such as the Impact of Events Scale (Horowitz, Wilner, Kaltreider, & Alvarez, 1980) and the SCL-90 (Derogatis, 1977), or the specific *event or the dimensions of one event.* These latter measures include, for example, the Schedule of Recent Experiences (Rahe, 1974), the Hassles and Uplifts Scale (Kanner, Coyne, Schaefer, & Lazarus, 1981), and the Vietnam Era Stress Inventory (Wilson & Krauss, 1985). Still others focus on appraisal of the event, such as the Perceived Stress Scale (Cohen, Komermarck, & Mermelstein, 1983), the Primary Appraisal of Traumatization Test (Segal, 1986), and the Secondary Appraisal of Traumatization Test (Segal, 1986). Although not generally considered measures of traumatic stress and coping, those that measure the quality and quantity of social support are also extremely important to this field of study, since appraisal of the immediate and long-term effects of traumatic events is so significantly affected by social relationship factors.

The Impact of Events Scale (Horowitz et al., 1980) is the first generic measure of PTSD. Several others have been developed, although none have been tested so thoroughly with the results reported in a leading journal.

Purdue PTSD Scale. One measure, however, the Purdue

PTSD Scale (Harris, 1988), has great promise for becoming the instrument of choice in measuring PTSD. A copy of this measure is in Resource B. This measure is a fifteen-item self-report questionnaire that asks questions designed to assess the twelve diagnostic criteria for PTSD established by DSM-III (American Psychiatric Association, 1980). The PTSD scale uses a five-point Likert-type response scale. In this scale 1 equals "not at all," 2 equals "slightly," 3 equals "moderately," 4 equals "strongly," and 5 equals "extremely." The instructions ask the client to identify an event in her or his life and write it down. Then she or he is told that the first eleven questions deal with reactions to the identified event that have occurred within the past seven days. Finally, she or he is told that the last four questions will deal with her or his reactions *since* the event occurred.

Although the DSM-III criteria have changed slightly, I recommend this instrument because it appears to have no significant effect for sex, age, and race per se, and its face validity and internal consistency are good, ranging from .82 to the PTSD scale, .59 to the Impact of Events Scale, and .65 to the Brief Symptom Inventory.

Brief Symptom Inventory (BSI). This measure is also quite useful in identifying current symptoms of stress. Though longer, with fifty-three items, it too is a self-report of symptoms (Derogatis & Spencer, 1982). Each item is rated on a five-point scale (0–4), with 0 equaling "not at all" distressed to 4 equaling "extremely" distressed. The client is asked to read a list of "problems and complaints that people sometimes have." He or she is asked to indicate how much or how little he or she was distressed by each within the past seven days. In addition to a total score, it has nine symptom dimensions scores and three global indices (global severity index, positive symptom distress index, and positive symptom total). It has good reliability (.68–.90 test retest; Cronbach's alpha coefficients equal 7.1 to .85) and validity (convergent validity with the Minnesota Multiphasic Personality Inventory).

Estimates of Social Support Satisfaction. Measures of social support include, for example, those developed by Caplan (1974),

Procidano & Heller (1983), and Burge & Figley (1987). Since the major focus of this therapy is to develop social support satisfaction among family members, it is critical to estimate as early as possible the degree of satisfaction prior to treatment. One scale found to be highly valid and reliable is the Purdue Social Support Scale (PSSS) (Burge & Figley, 1987). A copy of this scale is in Resource C.

The PSSS was developed to address the type and source of personal support of a particular client or respondent. In addition to identifying to whom the client turns in time of need (who may or may not be a family member), it asks the client to estimate the degree of satisfaction with each listed person's supportiveness on six dimensions: emotional support, encouragement, advice, socializing, tangible aid, and overall helpfulness.

This instrument is easy to complete, yet it can yield quite a bit of information about each member of the client's social support system and about the different aspects of social support. Moreover, we have found this instrument to be highly reliable and valid (Burge & Figley, 1987).

We have found that families with the best chance of recovering from a highly stressful event, even those that include several members who are traumatized, tend to identify other family members within their social support system. Moreover, they tend to rate the quality of support highly.

Family Adaptability and Cohesion Evaluation Scale (FACES). FACES (Olson, Russell, & Sprenkle, 1983) was originally developed specifically to estimate the degree of adaptability and cohesion that existed in families. (The latest version of this scale, FACES III, is available for a nominal fee from the developer, David Olson, Department of Family Social Science, University of Minnesota.)

Based on the circumplex model of family systems, as noted earlier, "balanced" families are those that avoid the extremes of high or low cohesion and high or low flexibility (adaptability) and have been found to be the most "healthy" and fully functioning in a wide variety of settings (Olson, McCubbin, Barnes, Larsen, Muxen, & Wilson, 1983). It is reasonable to expect that these families are in a better position to ad-

minister social support and to reach a mutually satisfying healing theory. It is important to identify the type of family vis-à-vis
this categorization prior to treatment.

Similarly, successfully treated families should have more
balanced scores than when they first sought treatment, and efforts to help families "balance their family relationships" would
be part of the treatment plan. This will be discussed later within
the context of the phases of treating family traumatic stress.

How and When to Administer Assessments

Obviously, you must see and interview the family whenever and wherever you can. Ideally, you should administer this
set of six instruments to each member of the system (testing
children six years old and younger will be discussed in Chapter
Eleven) as soon as possible after you suspect that you are dealing with a traumatized system. The assessments can—and most
often *should*—be completed between sessions without collabora-
tion among family members. The entire battery will take between one and one and a half hours to complete.

The results are quite useful in building the treatment program by tailoring it precisely to the problems, strengths, and
needs of each family. Partly as an incentive for completing the
tests and partly as an educational tool, we inform our families
that they will receive a report in a few weeks and that the results will be explained to them.

If a traumatic event was linked to the family's problems
prior to the first interview, the family should be asked to complete these instruments along with the standard intake forms administered to most of your clients. Doing this will allow you to
prepare more completely for the clinical interview and to form
some preliminary hypotheses about the family dynamics associated with the present problems.

I have found over the years that administering the instruments (other than the clinical interview) again every eight to ten
sessions and six months after treatment yields valuable bench-
marks for tracking progress and recovery. If there is any need
for crisis intervention or future therapy sessions, the data will
be invaluable to you or any other therapist.

Categorizing and Diagnosing Family Clients

It might be useful to return briefly to the model presented in Chapter Two. Administering the clinical interview and some or all of the standardized paper-and-pencil measures to our clients provides extremely important information. Among other things, these assessments tell us about how the family members are functioning under what conditions and the elements that would be most useful in a treatment program. Equally important, the assessments tell us about the family system's stressors, resources, and prognosis for recovery.

Attending just to the family system, for example, the Traumagram Questionnaire, Purdue PTSD Scale, and BSI provide a baseline measure of the collective amounts of distress being experienced in the family. Referring to the model, it is an indication of both the T (trauma) and the S_n (post-traumatic stressors) as well as the S_1 (stressors in place *prior* to the most recent traumatic event). It provides us with some indication of the extent to which the family has been burdened by stress and provides a good baseline comparison of the impact of our intervention.

The PSSS provides an assessment of the R_1 and R_2 (resources of the family prior to and following the traumatic event), since it is assumed that these parameters do not change much over time. However, a major goal of helping traumatized families in my empowerment approach is more fully developing the family's natural resources such as social supportiveness and family relations skills.

Finally, FACES III provides a good profile of the family's current functioning, or A (the level of adaptation to the trauma). It too will serve as a good baseline for treatment. I attempt to help the family become more functional by more effectively balancing their cohesion and adaptability.

We will return to the family functioning model at the end of the next chapter. It provides a fairly detailed overview of my approach to helping or empowering traumatized families through five separate phases. The subsequent chapters describe each of these phases in much more detail.

CHAPTER 5

Therapeutic Objectives and Overview of the Five Treatment Phases

You might ask at this point, "So, how *do* you help traumatized families?" Simply put, I try to create the most conducive therapeutic environment possible and attempt to *empower* the family to help themselves. In this chapter and the five to follow I will describe how I do this.

I have found that working with traumatized families is extremely rewarding. Most of my cases are referrals from other psychotherapists. Many of these colleagues felt that their progress with these clients slowed or got stuck. I suspect that for some the cases were too depressing and frustrating.

For colleagues who are interested, I urge them to keep working with their client family and allow me to serve them as a consultant. I assume a similar role with my senior doctoral students and the therapists I supervise in training. In this role I collaborate with the attending therapist by receiving a detailed description of the case, answering any questions about diagnosis and prognosis, and giving suggestions about where to go next. In most cases I try to describe my approach to helping traumatized families, but I also try to avoid suggesting that this is the only or the best way to help. Indeed, I decided to write this book partly as a way of enabling my colleagues, students, and trainees more effectively to help traumatized families.

Empowering families to enable them to recover on their

own from trauma is the most fundamental goal of my work with any families, but particularly traumatized ones. Most often these families would not seek professional help were it not for exposure to extraordinarily stressful events. Far from being "professional clients," these families are often extremely uncomfortable seeking help from a professional. They want quick solutions with a minimal amount of risk and sacrifice. At the same time, they often appear in the initial interview as a group of people who are discouraged, fearful, upset, and suspicious. I try to quickly position myself as their respectful advocate who appreciates their pain and is optimistic about recovery.

Treatment Objectives

In order to reach this fundamental goal, I attempt to attain eight separate objectives. I have found that these treatment objectives are valid irrespective of the presenting problem and the cause of the psychological/system trauma. This assumes, of course, that certain preconditions apply, as noted in Chapter Three. These objectives are (1) building rapport and trust between the therapist and the client family, (2) clarifying the therapist's role, (3) eliminating unwanted consequences of the traumatic experiences, (4) building family social supportiveness, (5) developing new rules and skills of family communication, (6) promoting self-disclosure, (7) recapitulating the traumatic events, and (8) building a family healing theory.

Building Rapport and Trust. A basic ingredient to effective helping is the degree of rapport and trust between the helper and the helpee. This is especially so with traumatized families. Some therapists have a special gift for establishing rapport and trust very early in the treatment program. Yet, because of the special nature of traumatized families, even the most gifted therapist may be challenged. Therapists are challenged by the family's general sense of mistrust in those who have not experienced the intensity and apparently unique experiences of the traumatic event and subsequent stressors.

The Murrays, for example, had anticipated that the focus

of treatment would be on their daughter and her potential suicide. As it became clear that this was less a problem and more a
symptom of a traumatized family, the goals of treatment shifted
to the system and the father's war experiences and postwar readjustment problems. This shift emerged primarily because of
the trust and rapport established early in the therapy program,
which were made possible because of both the clinical skill of
the practitioner and his knowledge of PTSD and combat-related
stressors.

Each psychotherapist must utilize his or her own methods. Since the method of treatment that is explicated here is
one of empowerment, however, it should be pointed out to the
clients that: (1) in most cases the actual therapy will be relatively brief, (2) the role of the therapist is to *facilitate* recovery
and self-reliance, (3) the task of the family is to refine and develop their own skills for coping with extraordinary circumstances, (4) success not only will improve current circumstances
but also will enable the family to more successfully cope with
future ordeals, and (5) they can individually and as a family be
useful to others attempting to cope with similar trauma.

Beyond testimonials and reassuring statements of purpose,
however, the therapist must *demonstrate* the utility of this approach in order to develop sufficient trust of all family members. This can be done in the initial or subsequent sessions using
the technique of round-table testimonials, which will be discussed shortly.

Clarifying the Therapist's Role. Another objective of my approach to helping traumatized families, consistent with my goal
of *empowering* them, is clarifying my role. I try to emphasize at
every step of the way that my job is to create the right kind of
conditions under which the family can find their own way, solve
their own problems, and "heal" themselves.

Over and over I have found that families—be they clients
or research participants—are unique. There is a considerable
range of functioning—both with or without a traumatizing condition. My role in helping traumatized families is to assess their
own unique circumstances and enable them to confront these

circumstances and thrive by effectively utilizing their current resources and developing the necessary resources to cope more effectively now and in the future.

This is easier said than done, of course. We psychotherapists have good intentions, but realizing these intentions is another matter. I always remind myself that each family has the capabilities to solve any of their problems by themselves *with the right kinds of skills, perspectives, guidance, and time.* And I have never been disappointed in my clients in this regard.

Eliminating Unwanted Consequences of Trauma. Rarely do traumatized families seek treatment without suffering from some unwanted consequences of their trauma—be they the classic PTSD symptoms that were noted earlier, unsuccessful efforts to cope, feelings of discouragement, or whatever the family believes is unwanted and linked to the traumatic event. Most often a desire to eliminate these consequences is the major reason why families seek help.

I try as quickly as possible to acknowledge these consequences and indicate that the primary purpose of any intervention program is to identify and eliminate these difficulties. Our goal in attending immediately and continuously to the symptoms is to both educate the family about trauma and traumatic stress and *reframe* these consequences in a way that allows them to go away more easily.

Building Family Social Supportiveness. Social support, or being helpful to another in a variety of ways at the right times, as noted earlier, is the most central function of interpersonal and family relationships. In helping traumatized families, I try to alert family members to the ways in which they effectively support, encourage, advise, and are generally helpful to one another—in contrast to not being helpful—and learn to be even more supportive. This is done through general discussion and in homework exercises that will be discussed later.

Developing New Rules and Skills of Family Communication. Typically in families unwritten rules emerge over years of interaction that prescribe the manner and content of communication among family members (Watzlawick, Beavin, & Jackson, 1967). Family rituals and secrets stylize and rigidify family interaction, resulting in a pattern of family behaviors that is generally functional in day-to-day activities. However, under traumatic conditions these patterns may be extremely dysfunctional.

A client family struggling with a sudden suspension of the oldest child from school, for example, had great difficulty in clarifying their goals for therapy. Rarely did the family members communicate with each other simultaneously about one issue. Mom was typically the alarm system for familywide issues (for example, an upcoming holiday or family visit or identifying a problem requiring solution); Dad ensured the three children attended to the issues and declared when the issue was dealt with effectively. Unfortunately, Mom refused to acknowledge the transgression of the oldest son, Dan, and did not want to get involved. Dan did not take this situation seriously until his mother did so.

I try to make family members aware that the purpose of therapy is to facilitate effective coping with these extraordinary events in which the family has very little experience. Family members must become convinced that to do this requires extraordinary methods (rules and communication skills), which they can, if they wish, view as temporary until the problem is solved.

New family rules and communication skills involve those that encourage the free exchange of ideas in a clear and efficient manner. A portion of the family therapy sessions and subsequent homework should involve teaching these new interaction methods. Several approaches have proven effective with families (see Guerney, 1977; Miller, Nunnally, & Wackman, 1975).

Promoting Self-Disclosure. With new rules and skills for encouraging self-disclosures among all family members, therapists should reserve sufficient time to ensure that all family members talk about their feelings. This reinforces both the rules and skills, and, more important, the hidden insights, feelings, and fears of all family members are more likely to be exposed and dealt with effectively. In the process of disclosing the various views of the trauma and its wake within the family system, family members tap their own creative problem-solving resources.

An example is the Kelly family (Mary and Don and their children Susan, eleven, and Mike, nine), who sought help in coping with the tragedy of a stillborn baby eight months into pregnancy. Everyone on both sides of the family had looked forward to the birth. Disappointed in their efforts to grieve the death of the baby, the family sought the services of a grief counselor six months following the tragedy.

The family was shocked to learn that Mike felt some guilt over the death. He felt that he was partly to blame because he felt jealousy and, thus, anger toward the gestating baby for dominating his parents' attention during the pregnancy. He had had numerous nightmares following the miscarriage, but at the time they occurred he could not disclose that the nightmares were associated with his once-felt anger and jealousy. By disclosing these feelings and experiences, he enabled the parents to express their own grief, acceptance of his grief, guilt and other feelings, and forgiveness of his normal feelings of rivalry toward a sibling.

Susan, it was discovered, had denied her feelings and attempted to avoid thinking about the trauma in hopes of avoiding the emotional pain and helping her parents recover. It was important to relieve her of such adult responsibilities and give her permission to grieve.

One of the objectives of this program is to create a context for allowing the free expression of emotions and experiences among all family members about anything they view as relevant to their situation.

Recapitulating Traumatic Events. Therapists should encourage each family member to articulate his or her experiences and feelings associated with the traumatic event in as much detail as possible. For example, therapists can encourage family members to talk about what kind of day it was when they first learned of the event, what they were wearing, and what they did and felt during and following their learning of the event. This will trigger new information, insights, and conclusions. For the entire family as well as the identified victim, this will reinforce the idea that the whole family was affected by the event and that the identified victim is important to everyone.

As the individual family member's stories are told about how each experienced the traumatic event and its wake, a picture of the family trauma will emerge: for example, that all were quite upset and worried and tried to cope in their own ways. Which of these coping attempts helped or did not help? What efforts did more harm than good, compounding the stress for the traumatized person as well as other family members?

The objective here is to encourage a retelling of the experiences connected to both the trauma and its emotional wake. Having the entire family listen to the stories of each family member causes new insights to emerge that lead to important alterations in the perception of the situation. Specifically, the family begins to develop a consensus view that can answer the fundamental victim questions: What happened? Why did it happen? How did each family member react initially and subsequently? Will everyone be able to cope if something like this happens again? These perceptions inevitably lead to greater acceptance, as well as understanding, of past and present behavior and attitudes of fellow family members.

For example, as the Murray family began to identify the initial period of their efforts to help Mr. Murray, daughter Tammy recalled how worried she was about her father. In an effort to "get his mind off Vietnam" one Sunday, she insisted that he take her to the movies. However, because of her insistence, he accused her of being "a spoiled brat." The use of rituals described by Erickson (1989) is an especially effective method for using recapitulation and integration of the traumatic experiences.

Building a Family Healing Theory. Others (for example, Figley, 1979, 1983; Horowitz, 1986) have noted that people who have been traumatized work through their experiences by developing new realities about the causes and circumstances of the traumatic event; they build a "healing theory" that fully accounts for what, why, and how it happened and why they acted as they did. A critical objective in this approach is to help each family member articulate his or her own individual healing theory. Then the therapist can begin to help the family build a family healing theory from the collection of family members' stories and theories. It is critical that the therapist allow the family to struggle with the various views of the trauma and its wake and the collective meanings of family members.

This objective of developing a family healing theory, then, is building a new, more optimistic perspective. It is a set of statements about the circumstances and consequences of the trauma for the family and an optimistic scenario of what would happen if a similar traumatic event took place again. Every family member will *not* embrace this consensus view (family healing theory) with equal enthusiasm. Yet it is essential that every family member recognize the need for such a view and be willing to support it for the common welfare of the family. To achieve this consensus, the family healing theory may need to be rather general and avoid language that is controversial.

To identify a set of objectives for a treatment program is important. It suggests where you want to be when you are done. However, reaching this end point is a struggle for many families. Before discussing this struggle, it is important to discuss the approach we take to adequately assess and diagnose the family. Such an effort is critical to both identifying families who are indeed traumatized and then designing a treatment program best suited to ensure their reaching the treatment objectives.

Five-Phase Approach to Helping: An Overview

The purpose of my approach to helping traumatized families is first to help the family eliminate the unwanted consequences of being traumatized and empower the family to deal more effectively with past and future stressors. As the family begins to function as they would have done were it not for these traumatic events, the self-esteem of the family as a whole and its members in particular is restored.

In addition, this approach rebuilds rapport and trust among family members. I try to help the families, if necessary, develop new rules and skills of family communication and thereby promote self-disclosure. In the process I try to help the traumatized families to develop a "family healing theory" to effectively handle current and future traumatic stressors.

Before describing my empowering approach, I believe it would be useful to provide a brief overview in order to get a sense of how each phase of treatment fits with the others. As you begin to use this approach with your own client families, you may wish to refer to Figure 3 as a guide.

Figure 3. Five-Phase Approach to Helping Traumatized Families.

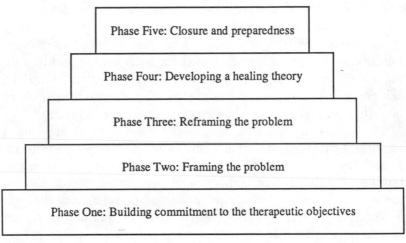

Phase Five: Closure and preparedness

Phase Four: Developing a healing theory

Phase Three: Reframing the problem

Phase Two: Framing the problem

Phase One: Building commitment to the therapeutic objectives

As illustrated in Figure 3, this five-phase approach first builds commitment (Phase One) from all members of the traumatized family to work with me to reach agreed-on objectives. These objectives, of course, include but are not limited to those set forth in the first paragraph. Without a minimal degree of commitment from the family, it is unwise to proceed to Phase Two, or to any of the later phases. But once the foundation of commitment has been laid, we can go on to framing the current presenting problem perceived by the family.

In the second phase the client family is encouraged to tell its story, especially the things in the family's life that are unpleasant and require changing. These things most often include a wide variety of hardships and symptoms associated with a family member's post-traumatic stress disorder (PTSD) and the breakdown and dysfunction of the family system associated with PTSD.

Once the problems are identified to the satisfaction of all family members who wish to be considered clients, the third phase of the treatment program involves *reframing* the problem. This means that the family discovers, or is introduced to, ways of thinking about its predicament that are more tolerable and adaptable for family functioning. These new insights or perceptions usually include the basic ingredients for a family healing theory.

For the Murrays, reframing the problem of Tammy's potential suicide included the perception that she was desperately attempting to save her family through self-sacrifice, that she was bringing attention to herself to highlight the challenges faced by other family members during the past several weeks. This self-sacrifice was a sign of love and concern in a desperate appeal for help from the people she loved.

The reactions of Tammy's brother and parents showed that they loved her and cared for her welfare. In the end, the family discovered that it was out of Tammy's love for them that she considered sacrificing her own life. This reframing of the problem allowed all family members to reconsider the current situation. Doing so allowed them to become interested not only in ensuring that Tammy did not commit suicide but also in identifying and managing the family's pressures and stressors effectively.

The next building block, Phase IV, is developing a healing theory. Like any theory, it consists of a set of propositions about a particular situation that is useful in both explaining the current predicament and need for assistance *and* predicting future outcomes. Through a continuing discussion among family members, such a theory emerges. Though less elegant than most scientific theories, a family's healing theory provides a semantic antidote to or medicine for treating and "curing" the trauma "infecting" the family system.

For the Murray family their healing theory would involve the imposed injustices of postwar emotional adjustment endured by the father, the pressures of dual-career families, and the extraordinary stressors of teenagers, culminating in a display of love and caring with the family system among family members.

For the Murrays and for most other families, discovering and effectively articulating a healing theory are the climax of a successful treatment program. Yet there is one more very important phase.

The final phase in this treatment program is bringing the intervention to a successful closure by ensuring that the family clients not only have reached their treatment objectives but also are well prepared for future adversities. This phase is either the hardest or the easiest. What is important, however, is getting client families to appreciate their accomplishments of successfully coping with an extraordinary traumatic stressor and to acknowledge that they are sufficiently equipped with the resources (both skills and attitudes/values) necessary for coping with future potential trauma.

Is it important to see the entire family? Some have argued that helping families means *seeing all family members in session all the time.* I see whomever I can whenever I can, wherever I can. I discuss the issues associated with unit of treatment throughout the coming chapters.

I have argued (Figley, 1984) that *most* psychotherapy practice involves treating family and other interpersonal relationships or at least dealing with them indirectly. A client, for example, seeking treatment for depression could be diagnosed with DSM-IIIR nomenclature as 296.2x, Major Depression, Single Episode. Estimates are that this client is not unique: 5 to 12 percent for American males and 9 to 26 percent for American females (American Psychiatric Association, 1987, p. 229). Yet many diagnosed as depressed link their malady with interpersonal problems, most often family problems.

My approach to helping traumatized families can be generalized not only to any family but also to any individual. The most critical component is the belief that there is some stressor or set of stressors associated with the presenting problem.

Now let us turn to a detailed look at Phase I in the next chapter. Here I will discuss the initial sessions with traumatized families and the process by which I enlist their commitment to the treatment program and its objectives.

CHAPTER 6

Phase One:
Building Commitment
to Therapeutic Objectives

As I tried to demonstrate in the initial chapters of this book, traumatized families often struggle with a large and sudden set of highly stressful situations. They attempt to cope as best they can and for one or more reasons seek professional help. For many families this is the very first time they have sought any kind of professional mental health services—either as a family or as individual family members. Therefore, the effort to contact and face an expert on family relations, as well as a psychotherapist, can be extremely upsetting for some or all of the family members.

Commitment and trust are critical elements in psychotherapy treatment methods. The early phase of any systematic, professional intervention is primarily dedicated to building a sound therapeutic alliance between therapist and family clients. Without it, clients are not only reluctant to change but also unwilling to take necessary risks. They need to be convinced that it will be worth the effort.

Most families who have endured a traumatic event or period in their lives hope that they can begin to put their lives back together as soon as possible and believe that this can be done by *simply forgetting about what has happened and moving on.* This strategy sounds reasonable, since the past cannot be undone and dwelling on it further appears to be useless and often upsetting. Yet forgetting it is rarely effective unless accompanied by a genuine belief that family members are now safe from harm and prepared to cope with any future traumatic events. Many families are able to gain this perspective and preparedness and move on unimpaired by the traumatic memories. Yet those who cannot will continue to display the characteristic symptoms of PTSD—both as individual family members and as a system.

Trust and rapport with traumatized families are thus especially important. When families finally decide to seek professional help, they may be quite reluctant to talk. Irrespective of their presenting problems with the trauma, they will probably be unwilling to disclose all of the details of the troubling events and the subsequent traumatic stress reactions unless they are assured that you know what you are doing, care about them, and want to help. It is important, especially in the beginning, to convey respect for all family members and an appreciation for their suffering. The therapist should allow family members, as many members as possible, to disclose their ordeal gradually and completely. Eventually their individual stories evolve and with it their goals for treatment. Simultaneously, their commitment to the treatment program will emerge.

Other critical issues that need to be covered at this early phase of treatment are the following: (1) eliciting the family's major sources of traumatic and post-traumatic stress, (2) explaining and identifying their methods of coping with these stressors, (3) enlisting support for the specific treatment objectives, (4) normalizing the symptoms of traumatic/post-traumatic stress, (5) noting the high degree of optimism for a positive treatment outcome, and (6) conveying a sense of confidence, authority, and experience as a therapist who has dealt with other, equally difficult cases.

Eliciting Family's Major Sources of Traumatic and Post-Traumatic Stress

Nearly all family clients will be very clear about what is bothering them and give some indication of how the problem or problems can be solved. The Murray family sought professional assistance to prevent their daughter from committing suicide,

for example, and believed that the therapist could solve this
problem by simply convincing the daughter that suicide was a
bad idea. But in addition to eliciting the perceived problems and
solutions, the therapist needs to identify all the major traumatic
stressors. I urge the family to list as many stressors as possible
that have been affecting them for the last month, or at least
since they began to recognize that there was a problem.

The interview with the family might go something like
the following. In this initial session, mother and daughter are
seeking my assistance.

Therapist: I can understand why you would turn to someone
like me for your problems. Tell me, in addition to these problems, what other stressors have you had to cope with recently?
You know, worries, difficulties, hassles, concerns. It doesn't
matter to me how large or small; I'd like to make a list of them
now. It will help me understand your situation better. Mom,
let's start with you.

The task is a rather simple one and allows everyone in the
family in the session to participate. I start with the mother because she is the parent, role model, and spokesperson for the
subsystem of the family. By listing the stressors, the family begins to recognize how difficult it would be for *any family* to
cope, irrespective of the circumstances. Moreover, it provides
the therapist with a clearer picture of the problems being presented by the family.

Identifying Family's Methods of Coping with Stressors

After the stressors are identified, it is important to ask
the family to describe how they have attempted to cope with
each stressor if they have not offered this information already.
Again, it is important for everyone in the family to talk. Together these lists (stressors and coping) will form a picture of
the family's efforts to manage the post-traumatic period—what
has helped and what has hindered recovery.

Equally important, the therapist is beginning to gain the

family's trust by showing genuine compassion, understanding, and acceptance of their ordeal, as will be noted later.

Explaining and Enlisting Support for Specific Treatment Objectives

As the problems, stressors, and attempts at coping are explained by the clients, it is important to begin to translate them into some reachable clinical goals. Although these goals or objectives may change, or others may be added later, it is important to establish a clear working arrangement with the clients about what they hope will happen as a result of the treatment program. Moreover, both the clients and the therapist will have a much better idea *when they are finished.* Following is an example of what the therapist might say in clarifying the current objectives expressed or implied by the clients:

Therapist: So it sounds like it has been a real struggle for all of you, that you want to rid yourselves of as many of these stressors as possible, get your lives back in order, and have some confidence that if anything as catastrophic as this happens again, you'll be ready. Right? As you were describing all your many sources of stress and all the ways you've tried to cope with them and thinking about why you came to me in the first place, I think I came up with a reasonable list of goals for us to reach during our time together. Shall I read them to you? Then let's take them one at a time and see what you think.

Normalizing Symptoms of Traumatic/Post-Traumatic Stress

Many families who seek help in recovering from a traumatic event are bewildered, confused, and discouraged. Members are uncertain if they will ever be able to fully recover from their predicament. It is reassuring when an expert at helping couples cope with trauma normalizes their situation and notes that their reactions are common and predictable. Indeed, a quite effective method is the use of "positioning" (Fraser, 1989): taking a position that is directly in contrast to that of most of the family's friends and other supporters. Most often, these people feel sorry for the family's traumatic experiences and urge them, one way or another, at some time or other, to "put the past behind you, forget it, and move on." A therapist might say the following:

Therapist: I can understand the advice of many of your kin in their hoping that not thinking about the event would make it go away. Sometimes that works with more minor events, doesn't it?

But frankly, I am quite impressed with how well you have done *in spite* of your ordeal, especially in addition to all the other stressors you listed earlier. I would expect you all to be much worse off. I am quite impressed that you have come through all of this as well as you have. Don't be too discouraged when the situation gets worse rather than better in the coming weeks. It's perfectly normal. As a matter of fact, it suggests that your recovery process has really begun.

There is a suggestion of regression in the recovery process. This statement provides both reassurance and normalization of the symptoms because often the process of recovery from a traumatic event includes this pattern. More importantly, however, it sets the clients up not only to expect these patterns but also to view them as a sign of progress.

Expressing Optimism for Positive Treatment Outcome

Another method of building commitment to the therapeutic objectives is placing these objectives and their connected problems, stressors, and coping efforts and resources into a more positive perspective. Family members are often quite relieved to hear an expert indicate not only that what they are experiencing is normal but also that one can recover fully from these symptoms.

However, I have found that such optimism must be calibrated and timed to fit the situation. Too much optimism too early may trivialize and minimize the family's ordeal; too little too late may have no impact at all. It should be viewed as seasoning for a dinner of therapy.

There are at least four ways of building optimism. These are reframing, comparing, positioning, and splitting. I will discuss each briefly and discuss and illustrate them more later.

Reframing. Family therapists often discuss the use of "reframing," or attaching a different frame or perspective on the problem. Indeed, an example is the use of "challenge" rather than "problem." This clearly relates to the systemic adaptation-to-trauma process model described earlier. The most critical factors are the *perceptions* both prior to and especially following the traumatic event.

But simply applying new *meanings* to heretofore traumatic experiences is easier said than done. Such meanings emerge gradually but can be greatly facilitated with our help.

Comparing. Another method of expressing or generating optimism for a positive treatment outcome and, by doing so, building commitment to the therapeutic objectives is the method of comparing. This is discussing one or more other client families who successfully recovered from a similar (or worse) traumatic event. If applicable, the therapist can briefly discuss her or his own experience with a traumatic event and the rocky but eventual road to recovery or the success she or he has had with families in similar predicaments.

I have learned to be careful with this method, however. If comparisons are not presented carefully, some families or at least some family members may get the idea that you do not appreciate the degree of distress and pain caused by their trauma, that theirs is not unique and thus not a cause for alarm. An example of what I have said in the past would be:

Therapist: I can see that this [traumatic experience] has taken a major toll on your family and each of you in differing ways. Had I not worked with other families in similar situations, I guess I would not feel as hopeful right now. But I have. It's like a prizefighter who is down for the last count, "eight," "nine"—and goes on to win the fight. It feels just horrible now, but you're not out yet. I can tell you have what it takes to overcome these terrible adversities.

Positioning. This method of expressing optimism may be more difficult, yet may be the most effective with some families. With this approach the therapist deliberately adopts an attitude toward the client family's predicament that may be the opposite of that taken by others who really care about the welfare of the family.

Often extended family members, friends, and even professionals suggest to family members that they should "put this thing behind you as soon as possible and move on with your life." In such a case I often display a sense of surprise that the family *has coped so well*, given the circumstances. I say that I would have expected them to be functioning at a much lower level, that they may even get worse before they get better, and that displaying stress reaction symptoms was *a good sign* that the trauma was closer to the surface—and as a result, their treatment could be more direct and quick.

Splitting. This final method is clearly the most difficult to use yet may be the most powerful with some families in generating hope for treatment. This method involves "splitting" with another expert's less optimistic opinion about the prognosis of the family. This enables the therapist to "voice" the family's worst fears through the opinions of an expert—a colleague, textbook, or media report about families confronted with the same set of challenges (for example, "trauma tends to destroy families"). At the same time the therapist can take issue with (or "split" from) this position because of the unusual strengths and characteristics of the client family.

It is impossible to say which approach will work best for which family. Moreover, one approach may work best with some members, another approach with other members of the same family.

Conveying Confidence, Authority, and Experience

My long-time associate and friend Wallace Denton refers to the wall in our offices with all our degrees, diplomas, and awards as our "credibility wall." Most often, he points out, the wall faces our clients. These credentials serve as important symbols for ourselves and our clients. They suggest, in effect, "you are in good hands; I am an expert."

Ultimately, the key to successfully moving through the first phase of treatment is convincing the clients that you will be able to help them recover fully from the problems that brought them to therapy. Rapport with and reassurance from the therapist are certainly a very important part of building this professional confidence. Therapists should also attempt to convey that they are fully in charge; that any extraordinary emotional session, setbacks in the recovery progress, or other ordeals will be handled competently and efficiently.

From the point of view of the clients, this sense of authority and confidence is often closely connected to the amount of experience of the therapist. You should not hesitate to weave into your interviews with the clients your many years of successful experience as a clinician, particularly one who has worked with traumatized families and individuals.

Conclusion

The initial phase of treatment is building with the family a strong commitment to change—to change from their current situation, which is undesirable but safe or at least somewhat predictable, to a new life that is free of traumatic stress. This is done by eliciting and emphasizing the family's major strengths and resources, identifying the family's attempts to cope, explaining to and enlisting from the family support for the treatment objectives, normalizing the existing symptoms, expressing and engendering optimism for a successful treatment program, and generating a sense of confidence in the abilities of the therapist to help the client family change and more effectively adapt to their traumatic experiences and memories. Yet all of us tend to resist change. Our least successful family clients have been those who sought a painless transformation ("You tell us what's wrong and fix it, Doc!"). Our most successful cases, however, have been clients who were fully informed about the course of traumatic stress, recovery, and treatment and were committed to the objectives of the treatment plan. At the least we need a strong commitment to the therapeutic objectives noted above.

Working with traumatized families is rewarding because, more than other families who seek professional psychotherapy, they are at a "teachable" or "treatable" moment. They are suffering so much that they are willing to consider some fundamental changes if they are confident that these changes will relieve their traumatic and post-traumatic stress and that they will be able to learn to cope more effectively in the future. Perhaps they will even learn to avoid traumatic events more effectively.

The Murray Family

As a way of illustrating the principles and phases of my approach I will include a brief section at the end of most of the following chapters focusing on the case of the Murray family and their progress through my treatment program. As noted at the beginning of the book, the Murrays are a fictional family, although their experiences represent those of most of the families I have tried to help over the years.

The Murrays were referred to me by Tammy's school counselor on the recommendation of a local psychotherapist. The family—John, the father, Mary, the mother, Tim, the nine-year-old brother, and even Tammy, the eleven-year-old identified client—were skeptical of the need for *family* therapy. It was Tammy's suicide potential that was the assumed problem and not the family's problem per se.

My task was to recognize their confusion and support their reluctance and suggest that we meet for "only a few sessions" in order to get acquainted. During these sessions I was able to successfully build a commitment to the *family*-centered treatment plan by allowing each family member to tell his or her story and come to recognize that the *entire family* was struggling with one or more stressors, that Tammy's problems were simply the most obvious to others and gained the attention of outsiders.

CHAPTER 7

Phase Two:
Framing the Problem

After building commitment to the treatment objectives and, thereby, the therapeutic program, I attempt to create a context for encouraging family members to disclose how they view their problem. Certainly, by now almost everyone has spoken about their ordeal. But this phase of therapy involves collecting more detailed information about reactions to the traumatic event. This phase is probably one of the most difficult for the family and thus is demanding for the therapist. Yet it provides the critical building blocks that will be shaped later in the program of treatment.

Memory management is the key ingredient in recovery from post-traumatic stress disorder. Thus, the therapist's task is to help family members recall the important bits of information about the past; then it is necessary to collectively help them manage, restructure, and reframe this information.

Families are a marvelously complex system, due, in part, to the fact that their members view the world differently from one another. There is no such thing as the family's view. This makes the task of memory management rather challenging, to say the least.

I find it extremely important to create a context that allows all family members to "tell their story," unabridged and unedited. This may be quite a challenge, since the views of one family member may be at direct variance to another's. Indeed, these conflicting views may in themselves be a major source of stress. Yet to tell one's story in front of the family creates an opportunity to witness and appreciate the feelings and experiences of other family members. And these elements will be extremely important in eventually building a family healing theory or explanation for what happened and why and in building a plan for dealing with future adversities as a family.

I have found it helpful to keep in mind at least six guidelines as I work with traumatized family members. These guidelines have helped me help those members who are trying to tell how the traumatic event or catastrophe has affected them and their relationships with other family members. These guidelines also help assure a more complete accounting of the past and current situation. With such an accounting the family is more prepared to develop a new, unified view of their trauma (that is, a healing theory) that will guide their psychosocial recovery.

Guideline 1: Telling the Family's Story

Rather simply, the first guideline is to urge everyone in the family to tell their whole story. From their perspective, what happened? What did they do during and following the most upsetting moments of the event? What were their feelings at these times? How are things now—better, worse, or the same? What are their hopes and fears for themselves and for their family?

Even though the traumatic event may have affected one family member more than another, as noted earlier, *everyone* in the family experiences the trauma to some degree and is part of the recovery process. Each family member who is capable (including children over six years old and those old enough to benefit from the experience) should be involved. Each is given an opportunity (and strongly urged) to describe in his or her own way the experiences, reactions, and views from his or her own perspective *without editing.*

Often these personal family member disclosures are extremely upsetting to other family members. This upset may be due simply to empathy, feeling bad for the suffering of this person, particularly a child. But it also may be associated with disclosing family secrets (for example, the father used drugs once, the mother had an affair, or an uncle molested a family member) or a point of view about the traumatic event that reflects poorly on another family member. For example, a wife notes how alone she felt after their physician told her and her husband of her miscarriage and that she felt abandoned by her husband.

The therapist's task is to praise any attempts by family members to shift attention from seeing only one victim in the family to viewing the *entire family as being victimized.* Family members should be encouraged (but not lectured) to examine the traumatic event that has disrupted family routine, to view themselves as having been deprived of the benefits of a normal family life due to the events and circumstances surrounding the trauma, and to rally together as a family to help each other overcome this tragedy.

In an effort to identify the full extent of the consequences of the traumatic event, each family member is encouraged to briefly (in five to eight minutes) talk about what the traumatic event *means to him or her as a person and how his or her life has been disrupted.* By assuring that these testimonials will be given and received in a positive way (rather than allowing them to lapse into a blaming session), the therapist assures the individuals that the experience will be quite productive. For example, nine-year-old Tim Murray disclosed: "I can't talk about my baseball game because Daddy keeps talking about the war."

The therapist asked at this point, "And how did that make you feel?" This helped the son identify the feelings he had related to these circumstances, and he went on to admit that his father's attention was very important to him but he understood that it takes time to feel better about something that was very scary.

It is often necessary to establish strict ground rules about interrupting another family member's story. If we do not do so, we risk restricting the amount and accuracy of what each family member will disclose.

Guideline 2: Promoting New Rules of Communication

The second guideline in helping families frame the trauma and related problems is associated with introducing new rules for communicating within the family. Allowing everyone in the family an opportunity to speak about anything in front of everyone else in the family, including a stranger (therapist), often violates the unwritten rules of many families. This is particularly true for multiproblem dysfunctional families (McCubbin & Figley, 1983a). I try to be sensitive to this variance, emphasize its importance, and be consistently supportive of those who attempt to follow these new rules, recognizing that it will be difficult. Anyone can speak about anything at any time as long as it is relevant to the focus of discussion and does not harm another person intentionally.

However, it is important that the family's distinctions between children and adults be strengthened. Thus, although I am in charge as a therapist in a session, I attempt to reinforce the authority of the parents by working through the parents to implement or carry out rules. If a child is violating the rules, for example, I expect the parent(s) to correct this situation (although I may remind the parent from time to time).

Following is an example of what a therapist could say:

Therapist: For the rest of our time today I would like each of you to describe what it was like dealing with this problem [use whatever language they use to describe the traumatic event and the post-traumatic period]. I want you to begin with the first moments right on up to right now. And it's important to allow whoever is telling their story to tell it completely and without interruption unless they ask for help in recalling something. Okay?

Mother: Are you sure that the kids should hear all of this?

Therapist: I'm sure. It's sensitive of you to be concerned about their feelings and reactions. But they are old enough to understand, and, from what they have said, I believe they want to understand what happened from your viewpoint. Is this correct or not, guys?

Guideline 3: Promoting Understanding and Acceptance

The third guideline I follow in helping families attempt to conceptualize or frame their trauma-related problems or challenges is promoting empathy, an understanding and acceptance of others among family members. Like the previous guideline, this one also promotes basic family or interpersonal skills. Specifically, promoting understanding and acceptance of fellow family members is not the same as *agreeing* with them. As one family member said, in rephrasing my long-winded explanation: "You mean we should try to understand and accept another's views as their own, but don't have to say it makes any sense or agree with it ourselves?"

The family is attempting to recover from a highly stressful event that has shaken the stability—and in some cases the very existence—of the family. Family members need to be encouraged to accept the need to hear the views of everyone so that they can both account for why they acted as they did and are acting now and, more importantly, accept these past actions. Obviously, future actions may not be so tolerated.

By establishing this and related guidelines in the family, at least insisting on it during therapy sessions, the family can more easily work as a team, work collectively to share individual perspectives about their common family problems. This will greatly facilitate efforts to reach a consensus about the adversities faced by family members perceived or framed in a way that will promote effective actions for coping with the adversities now and in the future.

Guideline 4: Listing Wanted and Unwanted Consequences

The fourth guideline I follow is getting the family to construct a list of the wanted and unwanted consequences of the traumatic event. I urge each family member to address these issues as they tell their story. But even more importantly, when the family begins to frame their situation, I find that such a list is quite useful. Here it is especially important that everyone contributes to the summary list.

I keep reminding my students and trainees that the antidote to bad memories and consequences caused by a traumatic event is the family's healing theory. In order to be effective, such a theory must include the few positive consequences of the traumatic event. These must be genuinely felt, not imposed by the therapist or only one family member.

The oldest daughter of a family of five was raped in her own dormitory bed at college. Friends with good intentions suggested that one positive outcome was that she had not been killed or needed hospitalization as a result of the attack. Though viewed as a positive outcome by others, the family saw it more as the absence of one more negative consequence.

There was one positive consequence that *was* listed by the family. Through the daughter's cooperation with the prosecutor's office, she was able to assist in the arrest and conviction of the rapist and thereby to prevent his raping again. Also, the attack brought the family closer together, and by doing so, or perhaps as a consequence, allowed the mother to disclose for the first time that she had been attacked as a teen by someone she had dated, but she had never told anyone until she told her daughter. The mother experienced great relief in telling her story, and the daughter felt a surge of empathy and acceptance of her suffering. It renewed their mother-daughter bond, which had been strained considerably through the teen years.

Guideline 5: Avoid Victim Blaming

A fifth guideline for working with traumatized families as they struggle to frame their situation is associated with blaming. There is a human tendency in dealing with highly stressful, particularly traumatizing, events to blame those most victimized (Figley, 1985b). This happens in the best of families with the most innocent of victims.

Frequently there is considerable animosity among family members toward the "victim." He or she is viewed, for example, as weak, unintelligent, incompetent, or unlucky. One of the goals of therapy is to enable family members to purge these feelings and, in the end, implicitly or explicitly communicate forgiveness of him or her. When this happens, the current situation shifts to individual family members' becoming more responsible for their own fate. Also, it is easier to shift from a focus on the victim to the family system.

A number of years ago I worked with the Wall family. Their story illustrates this tendency and a clinical method of dealing with it. Ted and Bonnie Wall sought my help for their seventeen-year-old son, Ted, who was having trouble recovering emotionally from an auto accident.

It became clear to me that both parents and Janet, Ted's nineteen-year-old sister, had not "forgiven" Ted for the accident, although they attempted to give the impression to him and me that they had. After sufficient information was collected and before we began the next phase of treatment, I asked Ted a question:

Therapist: Ted, what do you need from your family to help you recover from the accident?

Ted: Forgiveness.

Mother: Oh, Ted, how can you say that?! We've given you everything. We've . . .

Ted: Fine, thanks, but I feel you're disappointed in me, believe me—

Janet: Why shouldn't we? It was a stupid thing to do—drink and drive, you—

Mother: Janet! Stop picking on him.

Ted: I don't want to be treated like a baby; let me have it! I deserve it—

I allowed the exchange to continue for awhile and then asked everyone to level with Ted, and he with them. At the end of the session I asked them to not talk about this matter again until the next session. I asked them to write a two-page letter to Ted during this period (one week). On one side they were to tell him what they felt that was negative but didn't want to say until today, and on the other side were to write what they felt that was positive. I requested that they discuss their own feelings in the letter, to tell how it felt for them. I asked Ted to write on one side of the paper what he *believed* his family was trying to convey and on the other side what he believed they *actually felt.*

The next session was a lively and productive exchange that provided excellent material for the next phase of treatment. Briefly, the family tended to follow the same pattern of interaction established well before the traumatic event. This involved avoiding confrontation and disclosure of negative feelings, which, in turn, made others, in this case Ted, feel suspicious and frustrated about not knowing what was going on. Ted and Janet were the only ones who apparently disclosed their true feelings in the exercise, though the mother and father made some progress. By the end of the session nearly all of Janet's points (that Ted showed "irresponsibility, immaturity, and poor judgment," among other things) were reluctantly endorsed by the parents. However, we were able to reframe these apparent victim-blaming statements into ones that emphasized *behavioral* rather than *characterological* faults. Moreover, these statements were accompanied with feelings of love, worry, and care for Ted by his family.

Guideline 6: Shifting Attention Toward the Family

The final guideline I follow with families is shifting the attention of therapy away from either the identified patient/client or victim and toward the family as a whole. This shifting begins as soon as therapy begins. Indeed, the *fact* that the family was receiving *family therapy* and not therapy just for the "victim" in the family is an important distinction that family members should be aware of and be given credit for.

As noted earlier, families are exposed to trauma in many ways (that is, vicariously, indirectly or directly from inside or outside the system). In most cases the circumstances that led to the family's being traumatized involve only one of its members actually being exposed to a highly stressful event that occurred outside the system. Until recently all or most attention was focused on the victimized member. The family was viewed simply as "next of kin" or, at most, a source of social support who could be useful in the victim's recovery. Moreover, the family may have sought treatment primarily due to the victimization of one member and agreed to attend therapy sessions as a family in order to help this victim.

Gently but swiftly the therapist should broaden attention from the victim to everyone in the family. Although the victim may have suffered more emotional harm from the traumatic event, other family members have also suffered, and they require attention and help. The shift of focus can be illustrated in the following statement by the therapist who is seeing a family in which the father had nearly lost his life in a bad automobile accident.

Therapist: I am sure that Dad appreciates your being here to support his recovery from the accident. Yet Dad and I agree that he is not the only "victim" in the family. He is not the only one who has been wounded and frightened and is having difficulty recovering. As we can see from your own stories, everyone in the family has been affected in some way by this terrible ordeal. The family has been the victim of that drunk driver who hit Dad on the way home. So it's our job to help him recover from this accident emotionally, by helping all of you, those he loves, to fully recover and be able to put this nightmarish six months behind you once and for all and move on with your life. Okay?

Sometimes the victim is more than willing to shift the focus. Occasionally, this is not so. In such a case the therapist may need some time alone with her or him to emphasize the importance of a family-centered approach while at the same time eliciting her or his worries and concerns about shifting attention.

Summary and Conclusion

Our task in this second phase, then, is to encourage the client family to tell their story, to frame the problem. We are looking here for the building blocks for a healing theory, a statement of what, how, and why this terrible thing happened. We are also looking for a way for the family to deal with its crises now and in the future. We thus need to keep track of the views of everyone in the family, including their language, metaphors, analogies, hopes, and dreams.

These views most often include the unwanted side effects of being traumatized, a wide variety of hardships and symptoms associated with PTSD and the breakdown and dysfunction of the family system associated with PTSD. But they also include statements of hope, optimism, strength, pride, and courage that need to be supported, encouraged, and honored now and later on in the treatment program.

Once the problems are identified to the satisfaction of the therapist and the family (all family members who wish to be considered clients), the third phase of the treatment program involves *reframing* these conceptions. This will be discussed in the next chapter.

The Murray Family

As for the Murrays, in their initial therapy session was the first time that family members had learned of each other's unedited views about what was happening to the family. The parents talked about the pressures and pain they were enduring, much of which they attempted to hide from the children. This was surprising to the children. Though the mother and father were less surprised than their children about each other's experiences, it was useful information and helped them each appreciate why the other did as she or he did.

In turn and with more assistance, the children told of their difficulties in coping with the stressors inside and outside the home. The parents reported feeling both encouraged and discouraged by these reports. The father felt more depressed and ashamed after learning about the stress his children endured, partly due to his PTSD, yet he was glad that they were generally okay in spite of this and showed genuine love and respect for him. The mother felt a sense of incompetence, that she "should have known this anyway." Yet she too felt encouraged that the children were doing pretty well in spite of their pain and felt hopeful that things would get better now that everything was out in the open.

The new rules of communication were welcomed by

everyone, although Tim had great difficulty at times clearly knowing and stating his feelings and thoughts. This was particularly difficult when attempting to specify the "wanted and unwanted consequences" being endured by the family. A pattern that was present in the home was that Tim said very little, and everyone else, particularly his mother, growing impatient with him, would ask him a series of yes-no questions and end with a summary statement. All that Tim needed to do was move his head. By slowing down the communication process, Tim was able to take more time to formulate his answers.

CHAPTER 8

Phase Three:
Reframing the Problem

Just as Phase Two, framing the problem, was the most demanding for the client and required the careful attention of the
therapist, Phase Three requires the most creativity. Now that
the family has generated the various thoughts and feelings about
the trauma, the task is to reframe and *assemble* these views into
various compatible components of a healing theory. Also, there
is a concerted effort to directly face any and all post-traumatic
symptoms and reframe them in order to make them more manageable and more directly linked to the recovery process.

Although symptom reframing is very important, and, indeed, efforts to do this could begin during the first interview,
first I will deal in this chapter with the family's conception of
the traumatic and post-traumatic period. It addresses the fundamental questions that all trauma victims attempt to answer in
an effort to recover emotionally from their ordeal.

Reframing the Trauma

The precise approach to helping families reframe their
traumatic experiences and associated thoughts and feelings will
vary depending on both the family and the therapist. Similarly,
families reach this phase of treatment at different points. Most
of the families I have worked with begin this phase within the

first two months of treatment, but some require much, much longer.

Families that tend to be ready more quickly than others appear to be the most functional, happy ones. They are skilled in interpersonal relationships, enjoy each other's company, and genuinely like each other. The catastrophe they experienced undermined their faith not in each other but in nearly everything else. Many of these well-functioning families do not seek therapy and recover relying on their own resources. This does not suggest that they could not benefit from the help of a therapist, of course; they simply are more receptive to input from outside the family (for example, various media, friends, or colleagues). If they *do* seek treatment, they progress quite quickly through the five phases.

Dysfunctional families, however, were probably having problems—both individually and as a family—long before the catastrophe struck them. These families tend to have trouble reaching Phase Three and take longer in reframing their experiences toward a healing theory. Most of this chapter will focus on helping these types of families because reframing does not come naturally for them.

This step in the process involves attempting to help the family members reach some consensus about their views and, along the way, reframe their joint view in a way that makes it more manageable and functional.

I worked with a family whose only child, a two-year-old daughter, had been kidnaped for two weeks by a former baby-sitter. It had been two months since the child had been returned to them. Both parents had demanding professional careers that required them to rely on day care for their daughter. Both had taken a month's leave of absence and only now had sent their daughter, Candy, back to day care. They were both extremely upset about the ordeal and desperate for help in sorting out their feelings of anger toward the abductor, guilt about leaving Candy "unprotected," anxiety about returning her to day care, and were unsupported by each other.

One of the most destructive facts of the trauma they were experiencing as a family was that they blamed each other and themselves for "putting careers ahead of children." This shame played a major role in how they perceived the causes and consequences of their traumatic experience.

Gradually, however, they began to accept the fact that their careers were important to them personally as well as professionally, that their careers were a source of satisfaction and pride, and that the money and position they were earning would ensure that their daughter would have a good life. They slowly began to acknowledge that the kidnaping was a fluke that could not have been prevented. In the third session the husband summarized his position and that of his wife:

Husband: I don't think I'll ever trust anyone with her [daughter] again. There are some really strange people in this world, like the nutball who is now locked up [kidnapper]. And I don't think this distrust is bad, really. We know this thing could have happened to anyone. We're good and responsible parents. Maybe we will be even *better* parents now. We *know* what can happen, and we'll be taking extra precautions in the future.

Reframing the Symptoms

A turning point came when both parents realized that they had different stress management styles. What the wife initially viewed as a demonstration of her husband's lack of love for her and insensitivity to her feelings was replaced by a view of him as someone who has always had difficulty with feelings. She recalled, partly through the traumagram, other times in their marriage in which disaster struck and her husband, in her words, "turned into a computer."

Wife: I now see that he loves my daughter and me very much and wants to be supportive. He's just never learned how to do so. His way of coping is to roll up into a ball, emotionally, and hide. It's nothing against me. So when I see this happen in the future, I will know that he is having trouble coping, too, and not to expect him to respond as I do.

Irrespective of the functionality of the client family, most experience numerous troubling symptoms. These symptoms include but are not limited to those described in Chapter Two: startle responses, difficulty falling asleep, staying asleep, nightmares, flashbacks, guilt, depression, apathy, and relationship difficulties such as increased conflict, suspiciousness, and overprotectiveness.

Moreover, other problems emerge as the family attempts to cope with the traumatic and associated stress reactions—for example, a family attempting to overcome the hardship of losing a home and two pets to fire. As their home was being rebuilt they lived in two large rooms at a local hotel. During this period the family experienced a series of conflicts associated with disciplining their children, watching television, and general signs of dislike and anger shown to each other in addition to some of the symptoms noted above. The family needed to view their current difficulties in the proper perspective (reframe) that they would not be exhibiting most of these symptoms and hardships were it not for the fire.

So post-traumatic symptoms—both individual and systemic—are, of course, quite normal but are extremely upsetting to the family. In helping the family recognize and face these symptoms, it is important to help the family members reframe each symptom.

As noted in the previous chapter, the therapist should attempt to "normalize the presenting symptoms" as much as possible and emphasize that, indeed, displaying these symptoms is a *good sign*. Such symptoms are an indication that the nature of the family's problem stems from the traumatic event and is much more amenable to treatment than, for example, a faulty family system. Also, as noted earlier, in most cases the therapist should use the paradoxical strategy of "positioning" (see, for example, Rohrbaugh et al., 1977), in which the therapist accepts and exaggerates the client's position or self-assertion rather than the position of most others.

For example, when the mother in a family who was a victim of armed burglary and assault indicated that she was unable to stop thinking about the incident because it was so unexpected and frightening, the therapist would say something such as:

Therapist: Of course! As a matter of fact I am impressed that you are able to avoid thinking about it *all of the time* because it *is* a very frightening situation.

This "positions" the therapist as a strategic change agent for the family by accepting completely the family's views of their reactions and symptoms and gently introducing slight alterations in these views. Obviously, every case is unique, and it is critical that the therapist match the reframe to the family's own situation, language, metaphors, and pacing.

Yet, from the enormous research that has been conducted focusing on the personal and interpersonal reactions to traumatic events, we know that there is considerable overlap in the symptoms experienced by traumatized families. Table 2 lists some common symptoms, the most frequent meanings assigned to them by families, and suggested *reframes,* which may or may not fit a particular family but can be modified by the therapist to do so.

Table 2. Old and New Interpretations of Common Symptoms.

Symptom	Family's Perception	Reframed
Flashbacks	Haunted by past, indicator of mental illness, life-long problem	Vivid recall ability, useful indicator of "trauma work" needed
Depression	Giving up, withdrawing, selfishness, weakness	Taking break to recuperate, sign of caring, need for change
Guilt	Poor self-concept/-esteem, errors in judgment/actions	Courage, self-responsibility, selflessness, kindness, humanness
Substance abuse	Weakness, self-indulgence, hopelessness, impulsiveness	Effort at self-help, avoiding being a burden, need for support
Increased conflict in family	Sign of poor family health, lack of support, hopelessness	Sign of stress that would affect *any* family, not on same team yet
Acting-out child	Presenting problem, disrespect for parents' authority, poor discipline	Effort to bring attention to needs of traumatized family, sign of love, concern

This list illustrates the opportunity of the therapist to help the family reframe or "positively connote" what has been perceived as negative for so long. Doing so assembles a sufficient set of building blocks for the family to build its healing theory, the final antidote to working through the traumatic event and being sufficiently prepared for future adversities.

However, I have learned the hard way that *imposing* a reframe on clients before they are ready or imposing one that they do not agree with can be disastrous. I have learned to listen very carefully to family members and wait for *them* to offer alternative perspectives.

I remember a good example of a poor effort on my part to help a family member reframe an unfortunate experience. It involved a family of three teenage boys and a single father. The mother had died of cancer three years earlier, and the father was seeking help with the youngest, Jack, who had just turned fourteen. Jack had been caught stealing lunch money from another student's locker and while on suspension was caught shoplifting.

During the second session Jack had admitted to all of the crimes and was attempting to justify them by complaining that he never got enough of an allowance. His father had just agreed to increase Jack's allowance as long as he was willing to complete some additional chores on time and keep his side of his room picked up.

Therapist: So, Jack, perhaps your crime spree was unnecessary, but at least it was a signal to Dad that you wanted your allowance raised. Perhaps this will be the beginning of more open dialogue between the two of you.

Jack: Bull crap! I got *suspended;* I got a *criminal record!* You think that's work—a measly fifty-cent raise and then have ta' keep my room picked up!

Father: Jack! The doctor was only trying to help!

Summary and Conclusion

What I try to do in this third phase, then, in addition to avoiding egg on my face, is to encourage the client family to reconsider the circumstances. I gently try to get them to reexamine various thoughts and feelings about the trauma and its consequences and to reframe them and, thus, the problems or challenges they face. This means that the family discovers or is introduced to an array of perceptions about their predicament that includes a view that is more tolerable and adaptable for family functioning. Indeed, at least one of these perceptions includes the basic ingredients for a healing theory for the family in coping with their particular traumatic situation.

Returning to the trauma-processing model, I am attempting to get the family to reconsider the P_1 and P_2 (perceptions prior to and following the trauma, respectively). An example was the wife's view of her husband's reactions to stressful experiences as less a reflection of his lack of love and more of a lack of competence with feelings. Sometimes these reframes or changes in perceptions happen suddenly and seemingly without the help of others—a kind of "aha" experience. At other times they are introduced among a number of other views and are repeated and built on throughout therapy.

The Murray Family

Returning again to the Murrays, Mr. Murray revealed that his wife began to avoid talking with him more and more by going to bed and getting up before him. He believed that this was an indication of her not wanting him to talk about his painful war experiences. He slowly began to see that there was another explanation. She felt like a failure as a wife because she was unable to help him work through his trauma. Each time he brought up the war or displayed symptoms of PTSD, it was a reminder of her failure. With the therapist's help, he began to *reframe his perception of her behavior from a sign of rejection to a sign of love.*

Eventually, the entire family began to recognize that what they once saw as a tragedy and a terrible burden was a challenge and that they could work together to overcome it. They began to realize that working through this crisis together made them better equipped as a family to deal with future adversities.

Moreover, for the Murray family, the potential existed to reframe the "problem" of Tammy's suicide threat into the possibility that she was desperately attempting to save her family through self-sacrifice, to bring attention to herself to highlight the challenges faced by other family members during the past several weeks. This "self-sacrifice" was a sign of love and concern in a desperate appeal for help for the people she loved.

The reactions of her brother and parents were indicators that they loved and cared for her welfare. The family discovered that it was out of her love for them that she considered sacrificing her own life. This new "reframing" of the problem allowed each family member to reconsider the current situation. They were interested in ensuring not only that Tammy did not commit suicide but also that the family's pressures and stressors were identified and managed effectively.

To make this effort more concrete, perhaps another example from a therapy session with the Murrays might be helpful. In this phase, after each family member had described the ordeal from her or his perspective, the therapist needed to both summarize the progress made so far and help the family shift their attention to developing a healing theory by beginning to reframe certain key factors, to see things from a different, more constructive perspective.

Specifically with regard to reframing the trauma, the dialogue might have been:

Therapist: I am very impressed with all of you. You have told your stories well, and the others have been very supportive. I would like to ask you all to now help me try to make sense out of all of these views by first identifying the things everyone agrees on and then dealing with the others in the order consensus (most to least). Okay? Who would like to start?

The mother raises her hand and everyone directs their attention to her.

Mother: Well, it seems like all of us wished that this whole thing had never happened [laughs from several family members].

But another thing was that it has brought us together; we're closer now, and we trust God's judgment more than ever; our love for one another is stronger than ever [everyone nods their heads].

Father: On the negative side, I think that everyone thinks that I should have gotten some help for my Vietnam stuff a long time ago.

Mother: I don't agree, because I don't think you knew what was happening to you and wouldn't have known where to go for help if you did [everyone nods their head].

This discussion continued until the family was able to list a number of things in which there was complete agreement. The nightmares and more controversial issues (often between children and parents) had to be negotiated by the therapist and were generally issues that went beyond the traumatic event. One issue, for example, was the autonomy of the daughter. She felt that her parents were restricting her freedom because of the suicide talk. Her parents emphasized that her freedom had been an issue for over a year, long before the traumatic events began to emerge. It was partially resolved by a compromise perspective: that the parents had become even more cautious about her behavior outside the home and parental supervision, but that this might change if treatment were successful (that is, symptoms would go away and calm be restored).

CHAPTER 9

Phase Four:
Developing a Healing Theory

The final process of recovery from trauma is helping the family develop a "healing theory." As noted earlier, a critical objective of this approach is to help each family member articulate his or her own *individual* healing theory. Then, from the collection of family members' stories and theories, the family may begin to build a *family* healing theory. It emerges as a kind of antidote to the ordeal suffered by the family to date and will sustain their recovery into the future. Moreover, an effective healing theory helps in preparing the family for future traumatic events and, by doing so, enables them to avoid a good deal of unwanted consequences.

But you might ask why I have decided to call this a "healing theory." It relates to the concept of "trauma" as a wound. A theory, as defined by any standard dictionary, means "an analysis of a set of facts in their relation to one another; a belief, policy, or procedures proposed for following as the basis of action; an ideal or hypothetical set of facts, principles, or circumstances." To "heal" a wound or trauma, we need a theory or belief, set of principles or hypothesis that enables us to pose and answer the five victim questions.

In the previous phase the family members began to reframe various facets of their traumatic event and current circumstances. They began to reach a general consensus regarding the building blocks for a healing theory, a set of new perspectives offered by various family members. These collective re-frames were proposed in part by various family members and are important pieces of a family healing theory. Developing this healing theory emerges at this phase of treatment by building on the observations and perceptions of family members that have emerged over the past several treatment sessions.

Empowering families to take control of their lives and future is the theme in this and the final phases of treatment. I have found that in this phase of helping traumatized families, as they struggle to shape a healing theory, that they should be given more and more control over the sessions and that my involvement becomes more that of a participant observer or facilitator. This involves assuming some of the responsibilities of a consultant: serving as a sounding board for other family members; being a person who is objective, clarifying, and encouraging.

Moreover, in this mode of consultant, family members enable each other to propose a perspective of the trauma and its wake that fits for the family. Specifically, family members are encouraged to help other family members in (1) clarifying insights, (2) correcting distortions, (3) substituting new interpretations, (4) answering victim questions, and (5) constructing a family healing theory.

Clarifying Insights

I try to train family members to help each other clarify insights, perspectives, frameworks, and discoveries made by fellow family members and to refer to them later as they relate to constructing a healing theory or reframing some aspect of their experiences. This involves training family members to listen carefully to each other's views or insights in a nonjudgmental and caring manner, then succinctly paraphrasing these views for the family member in a way that demonstrates both understanding of the facts and acceptance of the feelings. This is often quite difficult for some family members on some topics. Often I ask family members to face one another and tell their story to each other, with the listener summarizing or paraphrasing what is being said.

An example is the anguish felt when a ten-year-old daughter disclosed in session that she had been sexually molested by her father's brother five years earlier. I turned to the father, who had been improving over the four weeks of therapy, and asked him to use his developing skills with his daughter.

Therapist: Dad, I would like you to turn your chair toward your daughter and ask her to tell you what happened. Use your listening skills and help her tell her difficult story.

What she told him no doubt was hard to hear. He later reported that it was difficult to concentrate on his daughter's feelings and experiences when he felt such rage toward his brother. Apart from his own feelings of inadequacy, anger, and frustration, however, he was able not only to clarify what his daughter was saying but also to express acceptance of her feelings and experiences. At the same time he was able to be as committed as he could to vindicating the situation and assuring that this kind of victimization would never happen again to his daughter by anyone and that his brother would be prevented from doing this again, especially to his daughter.

But by concentrating on his daughter's story, the father was able to identify some critical insights and perspectives that would be critical to the family's healing theory several sessions later. She had indicated that she had grown up during those five years, had successfully resisted her uncle's advances and confronted him, and in the end he has apologized many times and vows never to do such a thing again. The father's clarifications were just as good as mine:

Father: So what you are saying is your uncle was mean and bad and you were able to change him. It seems like you are a very brave little girl.

The father later voiced skepticism about his brother's change of ways, but the family felt some degree of satisfaction in knowing that their daughter had worked things out well for herself. They continued to struggle with the fact that they were unaware of her struggles for so long, with the newfound problem with the uncle, and with the other challenges they faced.

I have found that families always possess the ingredients for coping with nearly all of their traumatic stressors. My listening carefully to what they say and feel and feeding this information back to them and helping them feed back to each other enables them to work through most of their traumatic experiences. Moreover, they are able to *learn from their experiences* so that they will feel more competent and confident about future challenges.

Correcting Distortions

Family members are trained during the treatment sessions not only to assume (or reassume) responsibility for the skill of effective listening. They are taught (through modeling and guidance) to gently help other family members view various situations from a different perspective. In addition, they are trained to help other family members to apply blame and credit objectively or fairly. This is a basic family relations skill. Some parents are better at it than others. Most often, for example, mothers have more capacity to help children sort out blame and credit for their actions. This may be due in part to mothers' spending more time with the children, knowing them better, and, as women, being more skilled interpersonally than men.

As noted earlier, traumatic stress treatment, or temporarily coping with traumatic stress, is memory management. Here the family members are encouraged to help each other "manage" the memories by correcting one member's distorted views or conclusions in a way that will lead to effective recovery.

In the Smith family, the wife/mother was recovering from being raped by an intruder while the husband was away on business. The wife, when finally confronting the facts of the attack, concluded that had she screamed louder and fought harder, she might have managed to avoid the attack. The husband, taking cues from the therapist, was able to gently point out that doing so might have caused the perpetrator to become violent and attack not only her but also their sleeping baby.

This effort to modify distortions is much more powerful when it emerges from within the family system itself by both challenging and changing the original perceptions (in this case of the mother/wife's self-blame) and equipping the family with powerful tools for managing future stressors.

Substituting New Interpretations

Similarly, family members are trained not only to "reframe" various perspectives about the trauma and its wake but also to positively connote what is currently viewed as negative. These new perspectives are the final major building blocks for constructing a healing theory for the family.

The Smith family illustrates substituting new interpretations. Initially the father/husband appeared to be more upset than anyone else. Gradually, he became more and more supportive. After suggesting that it would have been worse for his wife to have done anything other than what she had done, he proposed a totally different perspective for his wife to consider.

Therapist: Mr. Smith, you mentioned just a few minutes ago that after you were able to calm down and deal with your own feelings of rage toward the attacker and guilt about not being there to protect your family, you mentioned in passing that Mom was kind of like a hero. Could you explain that?

Mr. Smith: Yea, well it's just like . . . Well, if you think about this the way it *could* have worked out, it's amazing. I mean, the baby was unharmed, the whole thing lasted only ten minutes, and the rapist was arrested shortly afterward. All of this due to her—[facing his wife] your actions. You endured this creep in order to protect your family and to be sure he was caught and off the street. You're truly a hero! What guts!

It turned out that this little speech did more for the mother's recovery than anything else to help the family's recovery. For her it relieved any lingering guilt, assured her of the support and respect of her husband, and reinforced a growing sense of inner strength and confidence.

For the father, it was a lesson in humility (his wife was not a helpless waif and could cope well in emergencies) and reassurance that he could leave town and know things would be okay.

This "wife as hero" interpretation became the central core of what emerged as a very effective healing theory for the family, one that sustained them through the ordeal of helping prosecute the rapist and dealing with the lingering traumatic stress. It reassured them also that irrespective of the coming life challenges, they were more prepared to face and cope with them.

Answering the Five Victim Questions

I have found that to be effective in building a healing theory, it is necessary to help and encourage each family member to work cooperatively and to show *signs of insight and acceptance of the current crisis and optimism about handling this and future challenges* throughout the last several phases.

Finally, it is necessary to begin to guide the family to articulate the full meaning of the trauma and its wake. This is done by asking each family member to address each of the victim questions: What happened? Why did it happen? Why did I, myself, act as I did throughout this ordeal? If something equally as challenging happens in the future, will I cope better?

As each family member *discloses his or her precis,* other family members frequently ask for clarification or justification. In the end, the family settles on a consensus view or healing theory about the traumatic event and its impact on the family. Let us review each of these fundamental victim questions in order to emphasize the importance of their answers and that they must emerge gradually from the family members themselves separately and for the family system collectively. ·

What Happened? The fundamental issue for everyone faced with a stressful situation—be it pleasant or unpleasant—is attempting to fully grasp specifically what took place. With sufficient information we then can categorize the event—threatening, nonthreatening, controllable, or uncontrollable—and immediately deal with the next fundamental question: "Why?" Often, however, we revise our initial assessment of what happened. We begin, for example, from our own perspective and quickly realize that more people are affected than just ourselves.

An example of this is the process by which an American hostage held against his will by a terrorist group revised his perspective of what happened. This thirty-three-year-old man sought out my consultation for three fifty-minute sessions. Our time together, however, was more a confirmation of his perspective of the ordeal than of any particular thing I said.

Hostage victim: Initially, I concluded that I was held hostage by a terrorist group for twenty-three days; that during this period I was deprived of my freedom, confined to a small room with my hands and feet chained, fed poor food and water, with no opportunities for exercise. I escaped and had to endure three days in the jungle until I was found by a local family. I was then subjected to humiliating interrogation by both the host country and U.S. State Department officials. I was reunited with my family in the capital city without any recognition of or compensation for my suffering.

Later I began to realize that my family psychologically suffered in this ordeal as much as I, since I knew what was happening and they didn't. They had to endure the unknown, various false rumors of my death, my premature release, and my culpability as "drug runner."

Therapist: How was it for them?

Hostage victim: After we were reunited, I expected them to be exactly the same as they were when I left them, but they were not. They were traumatized and frantic. And they expected me to be not at all the same: traumatized and frantic. Yet, by the time we were united, I had regained my composure, was able to get cleaned up, and had had a good night of sleep.

. . . Finally, I began to see that we as a family were victims—all of us—of some very nasty people. And we are in relatively good shape psychologically.

Why Did It Happen? Another fundamental question is "Why?" This, of course, is more difficult to answer. For some who have endured an especially extraordinary traumatic event, no acceptable answer is possible.

This is where faith and religion may provide a useful role for some. Although explicit explanations are important, particularly in being more prepared to avoid such situations, faith in knowing that the traumatic event was due to some divine will or plan is very comforting to some. Yet what works for one person may not be so useful to others, even in the same family. Thus, as a *family* struggles to search for explanations for why such things could affect them and not others, *one family member's explanation may be another's annoyance.*

There was the case of a family grieving over the death of a child. The couple sought marital therapy associated with sexual and communications problems. The first anniversary of their child's funeral was in a few months. In the second session, which focused on their marital communication system, the wife began to focus on the tragedy. It became clear that part of the problem was that there was little consensus about why it had happened. Both agreed about the critical components of the event: the child fell into a neighbor's pool after maneuvering both a locked door and a fence. The husband's only additional explanation of why this tragedy had happened was that it was "God's will." This explanation was not only unacceptable to the wife but was also part of the reason why she felt betrayed by her husband, unsupported in her efforts to recover from the grief because, as her husband suggested, her "faith was not strong enough to trust in God's will and let go of the memories."

Between sessions the therapist wrote a brief note to the couple, which said, in part:

The emotional pain you both feel for your son is real and equally distributed. Losing a child, especially one like Phil, is the most difficult loss imaginable. You have both coped as best you could. For now, John [fictitious], you have found comfort in your faith; Jane, you have not. It is reasonable to conclude that this pain and these differences are connected with your marital problems. It is now time to cope as a couple, as a marriage. For the next session I would like you each to pretend to adopt your spouse's point of view in coping with the death of Phil. I am very serious, and I want you both to be serious about this task. Call me if you have any questions.

The task worked effectively. Each was able to see the other's point of view and appreciate the need for a common view to emerge. Such a view evolved within the following two sessions. This view, which was to be the central core of their healing theory, could be characterized as follows:

We loved Phil very, very much. The accident was beyond our control, and no one can be blamed. Because we loved him so during his life, it takes a very long time to accept the fact that there *is* no explanation for his death other than circumstances. All we can do is have faith in God's help and guidance in moving on with our lives and the hope that we shall be blessed with another child who we can love.

Why Did We Act as We Did During the Catastrophe? The third victim question involves both culpability and coping behavior. Often our view of the way we *reacted* to a traumatic event is as troubling as the event itself. Moreover, our actions and reactions during a traumatic event make sense only on reflection, months or years later. Through this perspective we are able not only to answer this fundamental question but also to evaluate our behavior in proper perspective. We can recognize that we were attempting to cope with extraordinary circumstances (for some, a once-in-a-lifetime challenge) that would stress and overwhelm nearly anyone. Finally, by viewing our behavior (for example, symptoms of PTSD) in this broader perspective, we are given more hope that the unwanted reactions, behaviors, and symptoms will disappear as we recover from the trauma.

The task is more complicated within the context of the family. We must not only understand and accept our own actions during the traumatic event; we must do likewise with fellow family members. Families coping with trauma often focus first on simple survival; family members may behave out of character: rude, violent, petty, jealous, frightened, cold, rejecting, or short tempered.

In attempting to account for our own behavior, we also need an accounting of the behaviors of others. With this we can place the reactions of the family, as a group, in proper perspective and, as a result, understand these reactions, accept them, and, if needed, forgive them.

Why Have We Reacted as We Have Since the Catastrophe? Just as we tend to struggle to understand, to comprehend what happened at the time of the traumatic event, we are often perplexed at our actions and feelings *following* the event. Those exposed to highly stressful events are often dismayed by their inability to "forget about it and go on with life." Moreover, friends and family—and some professionals as well—slowly begin to promote this method of overcoming the traumatic memories. These unsuccessful efforts to manage memories—be it through attempting to forget or constantly ruminating about them—tend to undermine even further the victim's self-concept and self-confidence.

What is important at this point in the recovery process is for victims—all family members—to become educated about the immediate and long-term psychosocial process of recovering from traumatic stress. We must assure our clients that their actions are completely normal and predictable reactions to an abnormal and unpredictable set of events.

What If Something Like This Happens Again? Another way of posing this question is: "If something equally as challenging happens in the future, will I cope better?" This question also considers the issue of faith, be it faith in God, one's self, one's family, or all of these. The answer we develop builds on the answers to the other victim questions. Often we ruminate about the prospects of the same traumatic event occurring again. Even if we are reassured that it no doubt will not happen again, the remote possibility motivates us to think through our course of action. In doing so, then, we may analyze our previous actions and work out more effective strategies.

But again, answering this question within the context of the family is a far more challenging task than only being concerned with ourselves. The question then becomes: Will *we* cope better? Will *she* or *he* cope better? Will they be able to handle the strain so soon after this ordeal?

Indeed, a rape victim and mother of three seriously considered not telling her family if she were raped again, not wanting to repeat the havoc created following her disclosure.

Mother: It would certainly limit the pain suffered if I kept it to myself. Jack wouldn't try to find and kill the guy at all hours of the day and night. The kids wouldn't have nightmares and be afraid of every stranger.

Father: Yea, but do you really think that not telling us would solve things? Girl, you know that I would be even more upset if I found out from someone else. Besides, I have learned my lesson. I know that my number-one concern should be you and the kids, not going after the bastard. Haven't I been supportive lately? Haven't I changed my tune?

Daughter 1:   Yea, I'd feel you were treating us like babies. I want to know what's going on. I want to help take care of you like you always do for us. Wouldn't you want me to tell you?

Discussing the contingencies, irrespective of the emergence of a final plan of action, and reaching a general consensus about handling future catastrophes is extremely reassuring to families. And having such a plan is one more sign that they are no longer traumatized—they have recovered from the catastrophe, and they are in control.

Developing Healing Theory

Together, all of the answers to these fundamental victim questions, in addition to the many insights and new perspectives emerging among family members, can lead to at least a useful *first draft* of a family healing theory to cope with and eliminate their traumatic stress. Although it might be useful for you to *outline* the healing theory, for it to be most useful at least one family member must be able to describe it.

Traumatized families often attempt to rush to reach closure or consensus about a healing theory. A well-intentioned outsider, professional, friend, or outside family member may urge the family to adopt some pat explanation (for example, "God's will" or "it could have been worse") and put the experience behind them. Most often those who suggest these shortcuts feel uneasy with the family when traumatic memories are discussed.

I have often said to survivors that when someone says they should "put those bad memories behind you," they are actually saying "hide those bad memories from me." But even with traumatized families who are proceeding in therapy and working to develop a healing theory, the process can be rushed and, as a result, be ineffective in helping the family work through their traumatic experiences.

Sometimes a therapist or family member may become impatient with the progress of treatment. I have found that it is critical to slow down the process of consensus building (regarding the healing theory) and make sure everyone agrees. It might be necessary to go over the scenario several times to reach a point in which there appear to be no additions or corrections. Each family member must clearly be satisfied with the view.

It is not necessary for all members of the family to adopt the family theory with equal amounts of enthusiasm. Indeed, the children may not be as aware as the adults about the details and may even be somewhat skeptical about some aspects of the theory. What is important, however, is that everyone in the family believes that the family healing theory is a good working draft and will be acceptable until another is offered and accepted; that it is sufficient to keep the peace and get back to functioning like a whole family again.

Summary and Conclusion

Like any theory, a family healing theory contains a set of propositions, principles, and assumptions about a particular situation. Such a theory is useful in both explaining the current predicament and predicting future outcomes.

I am suggesting that such a theory can emerge naturally

in most highly functional healthy families. Yet even the most dysfunctional traumatized family can be helped to create such a theory through the guidance of a skilled therapist. It emerges in the process of a continuing discussion among family members.

Though less elegant than most scientific theories, a family's healing theory provides a semantic antidote or medicine for treating and "curing" the trauma "infecting" the family system.

The Murray Family

The healing theory for the Murrays involved the imposed injustices of postwar emotional adjustment endured by the father, the pressures of dual-career families, and the extraordinary stressors of teenagers, culminating in a display of love and caring with the family system among family members.

The Murray family's healing theory emerged as the consensus view of all its members. The mother was the first to put it all together. Her first attempt was altered by nearly everyone in the family, although more in form than in substance. This third "draft" was adopted by everyone.

Mother: We love Tammy very much. Although she really didn't want to commit suicide, her talking about it made us notice her sadness and, in turn, the sadness and upset of all of us in the family. Through these family sessions we realize that many of these problems began soon after Dad started having problems related to the war. We love Dad very much, and his becoming upset about the war made us realize how important he is to all of us: as father, husband, and friend. At first he seemed angry and depressed, and we blamed ourselves. We thought he was mad at us, wanted us to go away. We were afraid he was trying to tell us that he wanted to move out. Now we know that the memories of the war and his experiences as a corpsman had always bothered him and that only now was he ready to finally deal with them. It took him and us a while to figure out what was happening. We tried in our own ways to help. Most of the time we did not help because something like this has never happened before. We now see that these attempts, though unsuccessful, were signs of love and caring. We now see that Dad was bothered by the war because he is a kind and sensitive man who endured a very scary and depressing time. He now understands why he has acted as he has since the war and knows what to do if he has bad feelings about the war again. We have grown closer as a family because of this situation. We are stronger and tougher than ever and not only can deal with any other problems that might happen in the future but also can be helpful to other families who might become overwhelmed as we were. We are survivors!

For the Murrays and for most other families, discovering and effectively articulating a healing theory are the climax of a successful treatment program. Yet there is one more very important phase. Just as the reader of a great novel or viewer of a great movie may become dissatisfied with a poor ending, a fine and successful therapy program can become less so with an ineffective termination. This is the focus of the next chapter.

CHAPTER 10

Phase Five: Closure and Preparedness

As the family begins to articulate its healing theory and negotiate its precise conceptualization, they enter the final phase of treatment, closure and preparedness. This simply means that the family should be terminated as clients in an effective and responsible manner so that: (1) they recognize that the goals of therapy have been reached, (2) they can feel a sense of accomplishment for their recovery, (3) the therapist shifts from being their full-time therapist helping them reach a specific set of objectives to being a resource who can be called on at any time in the future, (4) they will be as prepared as possible to deal with future stressors, and (5) their program of treatment will be reinforced through contact with others similarly affected. As with the previous phases of our treatment program, this phase may begin soon after the family begins to articulate a healing theory and may last from one to six sessions. Every family is different with regard to how they welcome or avoid therapy termination.

Reaching Treatment Goals

At this point, then, most families will agree with and be committed to the treatment objectives. These include, as noted earlier, (1) building rapport and trust between the therapist and the client family, (2) clarifying the therapist's role, (3) eliminating unwanted consequences, (4) building family social supportiveness, (5) developing new rules and skills of family communication, (6) promoting self-disclosure, (7) recapitulating the traumatic events, and (8) building a family healing theory.

As noted earlier, this treatment model focuses first on the presenting symptoms and problems most troublesome to the client family. For it to do this, it is necessary to reach the first two goals (dealing with the conditions of intervention). In an effort to reach the third goal (eliminating unwanted consequences), the others are addressed either directly or indirectly. In the process the family system or network of interpersonal relationships is fundamentally altered, in most cases. This is accomplished in a systematic effort to reach the middle four goals. The therapist provides a good role model and establishes rules and methods of communication that may vary from the methods normally employed in the family.

The *effort* to reach these goals and actually reaching them, however, are not always identical. Most families at this point in the program would benefit from a systematic effort to reach the fourth and fifth objectives in order to resolve any unwanted consequences of the trauma, to resolve other issues in the family that may not be related to the trauma, and to be more prepared to cope with any future traumatic events or extraordinary challenges. Each of these goals will be discussed before dealing with the issue of intervention closure.

Building Family Social Supportiveness. During preintervention testing the client family's social supportiveness is measured. The total and subscores indicate the extent to which family members would seek each other out in times of need and, if they were to do so, an estimate of how satisfied they would be with the support. The results of the test yield a total score, a subscore of supportiveness from each family member and an aggregate score of support for each of the five dimensions of support (emotional support, companionship, advice, tangible aid, and encouragement).

These scores are useful in identifying the extent to which family members identify other family members as supporters, since they are asked whom they "turn to in times of need." Often those who have the most to hide tend not to confide in other family members. Moreover, the subscores for each supporter will provide an index of how supportive that person is overall. If a child, for example, tends to rate a friend higher than any other family member, he or she can be asked in what ways her or his friend is more helpful or supportive than family members.

The support trait subscores also are helpful since they indicate the net supportiveness for the entire network (all those identified as persons turned to in times of need). Low scores should be a concern to the therapist.

With this information a therapist is able to determine how far the family needs to go to reach a minimum level of family supportiveness. Often scores are a function of recent events that have severely damaged family relationships: trust, spontaneity, expressions of love, support and encouragement, for example. With most families, family supportiveness increases naturally as family members are encouraged to talk with one another in supportive ways. Thus, an increase in family supportiveness is a sign of successful treatment rather than specific and direct efforts on the part of the therapist to increase supportiveness. However, there are direct efforts made by therapists that directly affect supportiveness, including training the family in alternative ways of expressing emotions.

Developing New Rules and Skills of Family Communication. Again, the family seeks treatment because of a crisis that needs to be resolved. The crisis is represented by a set of unwanted circumstances in the form of various symptoms and other circumstances most associated with the memories of a traumatic event or unsuccessful efforts to cope with circumstances. Families are not interested in changing the family or themselves, although most will agree that someone or something needs to be changed. This they would like to leave to the therapist.

To suggest that the family needs to develop new rules and skills of family communication too early in the helping process is counterproductive. However, at *this* phase in the treatment program the family may be ready.

You might gently point out to the family in their own language how impressed you have been at their success in reaching some resolution to the trauma and at how committed they are to ensuring that they not become incapacitated by a future trauma. Suggest, then, that part of their success may be due to the way they are talking with one another.

Therapist: Ann, how did you feel when Dad asked what you thought about the accident?

Ann: I felt valued, like my opinion really counted, because he seemed to really want to know, and after I told him he didn't yell at me or anything.

Father: Yea, and it was good to hear your opinions about things. You always shut us out of your life. We never know what's going on. Now I can see that maybe it's the way we asked you—that at times you felt you were damned if you did and damned if you didn't.

Therapist: I feel the same way; you guys are great. But I am concerned that you might forget what you've picked up here. Because if you can continue doing what you're doing now, you can deal with *any* problem, tomorrow or next year. Would you be interested in spending a session or two on some basic methods (rules and skills) for improving family communication? [affirmative nonverbal response from everyone] It might be a good idea to go over them and practice them between sessions as well. It would involve learning a couple of simple rules and skills and then, after you are doing well, putting them into practice in real-life conditions. Okay?

The program can be one of many family communication skills enrichment/development/training programs.

To illustrate this phase of the treatment model, it might be useful to describe how the relationship enhancement (RE) program (Guerney, 1977) could be used. The RE program teaches a set of skills and rules that involve participants in taking turns being either the speaker or the listener or, if more than two family members are involved, one or more facilitators for the

speaker and listener. There are certain rules each role needs to
follow to ensure that all of the pertinent information is ex-
changed in the most efficient and socially effective manner,
which will lead naturally to understanding, acceptance, and
problem solving. Considerable session time, then, would be devoted to family skill building by practicing the skills under the
supervision of the therapist. When and if the family members
are skilled enough to deal with controversial issues, it would be
useful to focus on any remaining unwanted consequences of
the traumatic event. As family members increase their effectiveness in problem solving and coping in general, the need for therapy becomes less and less obvious. You have, in effect, worked
yourself out of a job! The family knows that they can call on
you again in time either as a therapist or as a temporary or part-
time consultant. And they probably will.

Sense of Accomplishment. It is hard for some families to feel a
sense of accomplishment in their struggles to overcome a traumatic event. Many report long periods of feeling "numb" and
near-amnesia. It is not surprising because, as was noted in the
first several chapters, families are often overwhelmed with traumatic and post-traumatic stress, in addition to their everyday
stressors and pressures. It may be quite clear to the therapist
that the client family has reached the treatment goals and objectives. The family may not share the therapist's sense of accomplishment. They may feel unprepared or not like they were
prior to the traumatic experiences, or they may have become
dependent on the therapist or therapy. In such cases I have found
it useful to place the family's current functioning in proper perspective, contrasting it with the pretreatment period of crisis
and confusion.

Consider, for example, the case of a mother of three who
had been widowed two years prior to treatment due to an auto
accident and had not remarried. She had sought out help for her
oldest (twelve-year-old) child, who was having difficulty in
school. It was clear that the mother was overwhelmed with pressures, only part of which were associated with the grief over her
husband's death. During the final session I played a videotape of
the first session to illustrate for her how far she had come.

Although the tape had been made only two months earlier, at that time the mother had looked years older, had trouble concentrating, was easily startled, and had difficulty understanding her children's perspectives. All this was evident to her toward the *end* of therapy. She recognized similar improvements in her children. This in addition to recognizing her achievements on each of the therapy goals reinforced her sense of accomplishment.

Therapist: You know that you and the children were able to work through the stressors in your life and finally bury your husband. You did it, not me. You have taught me the meaning of courage, insight, fortitude, and humility. This does not mean that you won't have setbacks in the coming months; I would be shocked if you didn't. But you need to at least pause for awhile and note how far you have come.

Note About Termination

As a family clinician for nearly twenty years and a training supervisor for almost as long, I have found that one of the hardest tasks for psychotherapists is terminating a case. I have used the analogy of dancing with someone at a disco in which the music never stops. After the third song you have had enough but think your dance partner may wish to continue, not knowing that he or she felt the same. Clients assume that the therapist will inform them when the "dance is over." And some therapists make the same assumption about their clients.

If clients know that therapy includes various phases, such as the ones described in this book, they are prepared for the final phase. Moreover, an intervention program that emphasizes concrete goals and objectives suggests, by definition, the appropriate end point for the program, when the objectives are reached.

Again, saying "good-bye" in a clinical setting is most often more difficult for the therapist, particularly a beginning therapist, than for a client family, particularly one that feels "healed." Thus, my observations here are more for beginners than for the more experienced family trauma therapists.

One of the biggest problems for beginning therapists is to

let clients go or, conversely, to allow clients to let go of them. Good therapy is like a good movie: it is over before we know it, and a part of us wants it never to end. Sometimes we need to have a "The End" sign for our clients. But some movies end too abruptly, and we feel cheated and frustrated. Our clients need to see their progress and be aware that the end of full-time, intensive therapy is associated with reaching the specific clinical objectives.

Sometimes, however, a client is afraid to stop therapy; concerned that she or he is (or they are) not quite ready yet to go on without the regular therapy sessions. Conversely, the therapist may wish to continue the sessions because, although there are signs of completion, the therapist (1) enjoys this case for one or more reasons, (2) believes that the clients need more therapy, (3) does not know how to terminate in an acceptable way, or (4) one or all of the above. My next book will focus on this and other extremely complex and challenging issues.

Some clients, aware that the end is near, experience a relapse: worsening or redevelopment of the presenting symptoms or experiencing new problems that require attention in session. This may be an indication that the family is finally willing to focus on deeper, more troublesome problems. Only now are they emerging, perhaps out of the family's fear that they will not be resolved if therapy is terminated.

This kind of "slippage" is quite normal in families struggling with significant change in their interpersonal relationships, and I try to convey this to them. Indeed, I often warn them that this will happen and that it is an indication that they might be changing too fast.

However, perhaps families are also communicating to us that the *end of therapy is going too fast.* They may fear that changing their routine of coming to therapy each week may be harmful; that they have come to rely on these times as a means of focusing on marriage, family, and parental issues; that they have become dependent on the therapist's contributions as a family member. This too is perfectly normal, particularly with traumatized families. For these families the shift in the therapist's role needs to be more subtle and gradual. For example, I often gradually turn my session leadership over to the parents and simply begin and end the session and contribute something only when it is vital. Changing the day or at least the time, if not increasing the time between sessions, is another way of gradually shifting the dependency of the family. Irrespective of the method, testing the results of these shifts provides a good indicator of the family's receptivity to terminating intensive therapy and of their ability to function well without it.

Shifting Role of Therapist

As I stated at the beginning of this chapter, the *nature* of the therapist's role shifts from that of a major to that of a minor player in the family's gradual recovery process. Contact with the clients becomes less and less frequent, eventually reduced to periodic phone calls or letters of inquiry about their recovery progress.

It is important to view the latter sessions not as saying good-bye but as celebrating, congratulating, conveying a sense of accomplishment. You need to repeatedly emphasize that your client family did it mostly on their own and that you only served as a helper. The family, of course, should be encouraged to write or call the therapist at any time but should be urged to use the skills and insights they have developed in session to try to handle their own problems as they emerge.

I have found it important during this phase to retest the family using the battery of instruments they completed earlier. This testing will provide additional data for determining the effectiveness of therapy and the need for follow-up. Moreover, if there appears to be some prospect of the family's being exposed to greater stress in the coming year, there may be some regression effects. If so, these same instruments should also be administered between six and twelve months following therapy and the family be invited to participate in one or two follow-up sessions.

Preventive Element

At this phase of treatment I begin to emphasize *prevention*. A critical part of every survivor's healing theory is the part about lessons: what was learned from this experience, and how we can better prepare for future adversities. In the final phase this component can be emphasized even more.

Most families will be quite receptive to this prevention motive since they addressed the victim question: If something equally challenging happens in the future, will we cope better?

As the family enjoys a sense of accomplishment for working through the current crisis, the therapist should pose one or more crisis situations for the family's discussion. This allows them to apply the insights and skills developed in the intervention program and to be given the confidence that they will be able to face and overcome future adversities.

Model of Survivors Element

As another method of reinforcing the intervention, the family could be asked to serve as a role model to other families seeking assistance. I often emphasize that they, by virtue of being exposed to such traumatic experiences and overcoming them, are now *survivors* rather than *victims.*

Some time ago (Figley, 1985b) I distinguished between a victim and a survivor, and I make the same distinctions for families at this phase of therapy.

The process of recovering from traumatic events is the transformation from being a victim to being a survivor. Victims and survivors are similar in that they both experienced a traumatic event. But while the victim has been immobilized and discouraged by the event, the survivor has overcome the traumatic memories and become mobile. The survivor draws on the experiences of coping with the catastrophe as a source of strength, while the victim remains immobilized.

What separates victims from survivors is a conception about life, an attitude about the safety, joy, and mastery of being a human being. Being a survivor, then, is making peace with the memories of the catastrophe and its wake [p. 399].

If the family agree to serve as survivor role models, they are told that they might be called on some time in the near future to talk with another family who is in the process of recovering from a highly stressful event. The family could be reminded of their feelings of discouragement, shame, confusion, and hopelessness prior to treatment. Such a survivor role model family might have been quite useful to them at that point, giving them hope and reassurance.

Summary and Conclusion

This final phase of the treatment program, then, involves bringing the intervention to a successful closure. Bringing closure is done first by ensuring that the family clients are aware of and celebrate the fact that they have reached their treatment objectives.

This final phase also involves ensuring that the client family is well prepared for future adversities. They need to feel confident in what actions they will take and equipped with sufficient resources and coping abilities and skills to ensure their success.

This phase for some families and some therapists is either the hardest or the easiest, because it involves saying good-bye. What is important is the effort of ensuring that the client families appreciate their accomplishments of successfully coping with an extraordinary traumatic stressor and that they are sufficiently equipped with the resources (skills and attitudes/values) necessary for coping with future potential traumas.

The Murray Family

This final phase was quite a relief with the Murrays. Both children were getting bored in session and were excused except for the last session. It was clear that this phase of treatment was for them somewhat anticlimactic. They had successfully recapitulated the details of their current trauma and related ones of the past, had recognized and eliminated unwanted family relationship patterns that emerged to cope with the crisis, and had developed an effective healing theory that would sustain them through—and indeed help them prevent—future traumas.

During the final session I asked Tammy and then the

father to describe what the family would do to cope with the results if a fire destroyed their home, or if Mrs. Murray were hospitalized for several months, or if a pet died. Their responses were polite but matter of fact and somewhat patronizing, as if they were saying, "Poor old Dr. Figley just will not let us go until he is certain we are okay."

Toward the end of the final session, I tried to develop a context for allowing them to return to therapy at any time without any sense of shame or defeat, while at the same time reinforcing that they were primarily responsible for effective adaptation and readjustment to their trauma.

Therapist: As we agreed at the end of the last session, I would like to see you all back here for fifteen minutes in three months (no charge). It will be an opportunity to talk about things, face to face, and to answer any questions you might have. I want to emphasize now, and I will again in three months, that you all should feel good about yourselves as people and as a team, a family. I have tried to provide a place here to work on things, but you all did the work. I do hope that you will be willing to help other families when and if you can. You would be great survivor role models. And finally, don't be concerned if the trauma flares up again sometime in the future. It is natural to have bad memories or to get angry or confused about the past from time to time. It is an indication that you are sensitive and caring people. Any questions or comments? See you in three months.

CHAPTER 11

Special Help
for Traumatized Children

Throughout this book I have talked about children in general terms and included them in most of the case examples. Because they are so different from adults and, as a result, so special, I have devoted an entire chapter just to traumatized children.

I enjoy working with children, even those who have been traumatized. Perhaps it is because children are so resilient, or perhaps it is because the reactions of a child are more obvious and less complex than those of adults. As I read the professional literature, I do not get a sense from the authors of the satisfaction I have experienced. Perhaps it is because traumatized children are so pitiful.

Certainly, childhood emotional trauma has been the focus of individual psychotherapy since the latter's inception. Yet only recently, however, has post-traumatic stress disorder (PTSD) in children received the necessary scientific attention to development of effective, verifiable, and replicable treatment methods.

In this chapter I will try to explain how I work with children within the context of helping and empowering their families. In my opinion, however, working effectively with traumatized children requires a clear understanding of child development and the typical methods children use to cope with stress, particularly traumatic stress. Before I focus on helping traumatized children, I will discuss some of these background issues.

123

Developmental Issues in Traumatization

My work with traumatized children has changed over the years, based partly on my professional experiences but largely on my experiences as a parent. As most parents already know, there are vast differences among children with regard to their reactions to highly stressful situations. The age of the child, the circumstances of the stressor, and the reactions of the caretakers are the major factors that determine if the child will be traumatized and the speed of psychological recovery.

Before discussing my approach to helping children and helping families help children, I would like to discuss the developmental issues associated with traumatization. These issues center on the cognitive capacities and psychosocial needs of children at various ages. Even so, however, not every child behaves like textbook descriptions. Children have taught me over the years to expect certain things but not to be surprised if I find something different, to be willing to revise my prognosis as the unique circumstances of the child and her or his family emerge.

Special Nature of Children. Most would agree that children are the most precious of living things. This is why most of us are profoundly affected emotionally when a child is injured or in distress. Part of this is due to our belief that children are blameless, innocent, and often helpless. Another is the belief that children will become more emotionally upset from such a situation. This is not necessarily true, however. What do we know and not know about childhood fears, phobias, and traumas? Unfortunately, we do not know as much as we should.

Our understanding and treatment of childhood stress and stress disorders are considerably underdeveloped compared to adult studies. Only recently have we begun recognizing a link between common childhood phobia and traumatic stress reactions, for example (Berecz, 1968; Eth & Pynoos, 1985a, 1985b; Hyman, Zelikoff, & Clarke, 1987).

Variations in Reactions. I appreciate Carol Mowbray's perspectives on children's reactions to stress. Recently (1988) she pointed out that to understand childhood stress disorders, we must first appreciate the developmental stages children pass through, particularly with regard to cognitive and moral development. Moreover, each stage is associated with varying degrees of coping and defense mechanisms employed by children and how grief and mourning are manifested in children's actions. From a comprehensive review of the literature in this area, Mowbray developed a useful table that summarizes the common reactions of children in various age groups.

Table 3. Summary of Common Victim Reactions by Age Grouping.

	Preschool	School Age	Adolescent
Fears and worries	X	X	X
Somatic problems	X	X	
Restitutive play, compulsions	X	X	
Regression and separation anxiety	X	X	
Nightmares and sleep disturbances	X	X	X
Fantasies		X	X
Anger, hostility, belligerence		X	X
Interpersonal problems		X	X
School phobias and other school problems		X	X
Apathy, withdrawal			X
Guilt, moral development		X	X
Personality change			X
Chronic sadness and depression		X	X
Self-deprecation		X	X
Intellectualization, including rationalization			X
Anxiety			X
Acting out			X

Source: Mowbray, C. T. (1988). Post-traumatic therapy for children who are victims of violence. In F. M. Ochberg (Ed.), *Post-traumatic therapy and victims of violence* (pp. 196–212). New York: Brunner/Mazel. Reprinted with permission from the publisher.

As human beings, we all learn to cope with stressors of varying types with varying degrees of effectiveness. As early as the first month of life, infants begin to develop these methods of coping with stress. New and more complex patterns of behavior evolve. An infant who looks long and hard at a new object before reaching for it is also the toddler who stands in the nursery school doorway and watches the other children before joining their play (Murphy & Moriarty, 1976).

Children's Methods of Coping

Children use a variety of methods for coping with stress— be it traumatic or nontraumatic. These include crying, withdrawal, fantasy, sleep, feigning illness, regression, acting out, altruism, identification with the aggressor, anticipation, denial, and sublimation. I will discuss each briefly.

Crying. Although crying is extremely upsetting to parents, it is frequently chosen by children as a method of coping with highly stressful experiences. It is a method of bringing attention to their anxiety and pain and needed comfort and reassurance.

Withdrawal. Children cope by removing themselves from reminders of the stressors. Moreover, by focusing on other things, they find relief from unpleasant, "scary and ucky" thoughts associated with the traumatic events. As Scarlett O'Hara said in *Gone with the Wind*, "I'll think about that tomorrow." Even when children are not physically withdrawn from family activities, they may succeed in withdrawing psychologically, appearing preoccupied, in a daze.

Fantasy. Some children cope by pretending they are somewhere else, are with someone else, or *are* someone else. Some children, for example, adopt fantasy friends or treat toys as real people in place of family members and friends.

These efforts of replacing real with unreal people can become extreme and pathological. Some suggest (see, for example, Kluft, 1984) that multiple personality disorder can be traced to a dissociative "splitting" of the self and another personality who is able or more willing to handle the traumatic stressors.

Sublimation. Another form of withdrawal is sublimation. Here children choose to vent and express their reactions to stressful situations by becoming engrossed in some type of activity. For some it may be videogames or videotapes. For other children it may be fantasy games with dolls or cars. These activities provide structure, routine, and predictability to the child at a time when these are most needed.

Sleep. Other children cope by staying in bed, taking long naps, or going to bed early. In the absence of nightmares or night terrors, sleep is particularly appealing as an escape from reality. Time passes more quickly during sleep. Some children feel more safe in bed and in a relaxed state such as sleep.

Feigning Illness. Some children cope with stress by becoming sick, either in a psychosomatic form or, more directly, by pretending to be sick. As with secondary gain, being sick is often associated with extra attention, kindness, and special favors. Moreover, when you are sick you are not expected to function or cope like people (that is, parents) expect, nor as you expect of yourself.

These special favors received by sick children are things that might be helpful for some children in coping with highly stressful experiences. They may be unable or unwilling to ask for these things as a way of coping with stress. Indeed, some may be aware they need special treatment, and if they do that the need is associated with stress. Moreover, parents may be unwilling to provide special attention for any reason *other* than due to illness.

Regression. Children also may act like they are younger than they are, becoming more dependent, demanding, childish, and uncooperative. A six-year-old may start sucking her thumb or wetting the bed. A three-year-old may demand to use a high chair or diapers again. Similar to the situation with illness, they may be seeking additional comfort, reassurance, and predictability in their life that only a loving parent can provide.

Acting Out. Another way of gaining attention and thereby avoiding the reality and consequences of the stressful experiences is impulsively acting out. This involves sudden and pur-

posive violations of family or household rules, school or community codes, rules, or laws. Often this acting out is an immediate way of shifting attention to the violation and away from
efforts to cope with the stressors.

Altruism. There are also positive methods that children choose
for coping with highly stressful situations. Children who suddenly become extremely helpful and useful to other family
members and friends bathe in the appreciation and love their
behavior generates. This too enables them to forget about their
troubles, bring attention to themselves, and utilize these signs of
appreciation as a way of recovering from stressful circumstances.

Identification with Aggressor. In cases in which children must
cope with an ongoing traumatic experience, such as child abuse—
inside or outside the home by an adult or a child—she or he may
display what some have called the "Stockholm syndrome"
(Eitinger, 1982). It was named after the young female bank
clerks held hostage in a Stockholm bank robbery who, after
being released, attacked the police and defended the criminals.
Like children controlled by an aggressor, they identified with
their captor so much for survival that they began, at least until
they were safe again, to display signs of affection and liking.

Anticipation. "What if you die, Mummy?" is a common question from children who experience the death of someone in
their life. By foreseeing and planning for other stressful events,
children feel more prepared and, thus, more in control of their
lives. Often parents discourage anticipation and such questions
out of concern that the preparation may be worse than what actually happens. But preparation rarely is worse. Children seek
structure, control, and security in their lives, particularly during
or following a highly stressful event.

Humor. Similar to adults, children use humor to cope with
stress: expressing pain, fear, disappointment, frustration, anger,
neediness. Humor takes different forms, of course, depending
on the age of the child. Younger children utilize more physical
methods, in contrast to older children, who are more intellec-

tual and complicated in their use of humor. Often humor is a means of distraction rather than a way of seeking some resolution of the crisis or stressful situation.

Denial. Finally, denial is one of the most frequently used methods of coping with stress for both adults and children. By refusing to believe that the stressful situation exists or that they or their loved ones are affected, they are able to avoid the costs of such a situation. Used in moderation, this form of coping can be quite appropriate for children. Many of the methods of coping discussed above are in varying degrees forms of denial. It provides a needed respite from overwhelmingly stressful circumstances.

An especially good example of how children cope with "traumatic" experiences happened in our household last year. When our daughter Laura first experienced, at three years of age, the absence of her older sister, Jessica, who was visiting her grandparents in Florida, Laura first wanted to know all about Florida (engagement). Then she chose to watch several of her favorite videotapes (avoidance). She cried for awhile, exclaiming how she missed her sister, when we refused to give her another piece of candy before dinner (mourning). Later we overheard her explaining to her "baby," Elizabeth the duck, why Jessica was gone and that she would be back soon (fantasy). Laura utilized a variety of coping methods to deal with a highly stressful, potentially traumatic event. I doubt if Laura realized that she had chosen these activities to help her recover from her anxiety over Jessica's being gone.

There are many classical methods children utilize to adapt to or cope with stress, including traumatic or post-traumatic stress. This occurs naturally, sometimes encouraged and sometimes discouraged by parents. Now let us look at some established ways of assessing children who may be at the greatest risk of psychic damage due to traumatic stress.

Helping Traumatized Children

Again, working effectively with traumatized children requires a clear understanding of child development, typical methods children use to cope with traumatic and post-traumatic stress, and the context of the traumatizing and recovering context.

The use of enactment, visual imagery, and other hypnotic and child-centered methods shows promise in treating children with PTSD. My position is, however, that treating childhood PTSD within the family context should be the treatment of choice. Treating children diagnosed with PTSD involves mobilizing the family to focus on the unwanted symptoms and thoughts.

Family therapy is not only a treatment technique but is also a relatively new and powerful alternative approach to viewing, preventing, and treating childhood disorders. Yet although children frequently are part of the family therapy treatment context (in the room with the parents), they are generally ignored by family therapists unless they are closely linked with the presenting problem (for example, adolescent drug abuse). Published reports on the treatment of traumatized children using family therapy are rare.

I believe, based on my own experiences and those of my students and the therapists I supervise, that my empowerment approach to helping traumatized families works well with children. However, my work has evolved from many colleagues with much experience working with and treating children. I would like to review some of these building blocks before discussing my work with children that might be unique.

Only a small minority of children who are traumatized by various events actually see a psychotherapist. Most recover anyway because of the way adults attend to them. Children exposed to frightening stressors, for example, require the calming and protective presence of a parent or, if at school, a trusted teacher. These sensitive adults are able to get the child to articulate the source of her or his anxiety and all of the associated fears.

Issues of Assessing Traumatized Children. My psychometric protocol, including the standardized clinical interview, as you can detect, relies on a minimal level of verbal and cognitive skill that might be beyond the abilities of some children, particularly eight-year-olds and younger. However, in most instances I rely on the parents to represent their younger children in completing the measures for them. I rely on my colleagues who have studied and worked with children extensively to alert me to unique assessment issues with children.

I agree with Mowbray (1988), for example, that a comprehensive assessment of the child is important as soon after the traumatic event as possible. Among other things, the child victim should be asked about all the details of the event and be allowed to answer at a comfortable pace. It is critical that children not feel in any way accused or blamed for what has happened.

Mowbray (1988) suggests that there are certain risk factors associated with the development of PTSD in children: (1) the child experiences the loss of a significant attachment figure (parent, pet, sibling, friend); (2) parents' reactions are extremely disturbed; (3) the caretaker's parenting abilities are disrupted for some reason; (4) the family atmosphere is chaotic, nonsupportive, or violent; (5) the child is physically hurt; (6) the child has been previously victimized or traumatized or has experienced emotional disturbance; or (7) the trauma was prolonged or involved multiple episodes or was not acknowledged until much later (p. 207).

Similarly, identifying children at risk is important when a parent dies. I have used the findings of Osterweis and Townsend (1988) as important markers for these and other traumatized children. Osterweis and Townsend have observed that the following factors increase the risk of long-term negative outcomes following the death of a parent or sibling:

- loss when the child is under five years of age or in early adolescence
- loss of mother for girls under eleven and loss of father for adolescent boys
- preexisting emotional difficulties
- preexisting conflict between the child and the deceased
- a surviving parent who becomes excessively dependent on the child
- lack of adequate family or community supports, or a parent who cannot use support systems

- unstable, disrupted environments, including numerous care-takers and broken routines
- a parent who marries someone with whom the child has a bad relationship
- sudden or violent death (including suicide or murder)

Child-Centered Approaches to Helping Traumatized Children. Terr (1989), in a recent review, notes that there are a number of psychotherapies for childhood psychic trauma. Among those she cites are psychodynamic psychotherapies, which include individual analysis, hypnosis, play therapy, pharmacological therapies (for both fear and post-traumatic memory), behavioral therapy, group therapy, and family therapy. Perhaps the most closely tied to children and successful treatment of childhood fears has been the use of play therapy.

Play therapy (ludotherapy) is the use of play activities and materials in child psychotherapy. This approach is based on the belief that such activities mirror the child's emotional life and fantasies. Play then brings out these feelings and problems in order to test out new perspectives, approaches, and relationships in action rather than words.

Similarly, Green (1978) utilizes psychoanalytically oriented play therapy in the treatment of physically and mentally abused preschool-aged children. The goals are to emphasize ego integration, reality testing, containing drives and impulses, and strengthening higher-level defenses. Green attempts to relieve acute, abuse-related traumatic stress reactions by allowing the child to master the trauma through repetition and symbolic reenactment using play, dolls, puppets, and drawings. His approach typifies the more dynamically oriented child therapies.

Consistent with my own thinking, Mowbray (1988) has noted six issues, drawn from the work of Raphael (1975), that should be addressed in long-term therapy with traumatized children:

1. Helping the child face the truth of what has happened.
2. Dealing with the "damaged goods syndrome"—poor self-image, avoidance of interpersonal relations, and so on.

3. Identifying guilt and self-blame.
4. Dealing with emotions such as anger, grief, and fear and how these may be expressed.
5. Helping the child to identify and access supportive resources—for example, who can he or she trust, and how can he or she protect him- or herself in the future?
6. For child victims of sexual assault: how to interpret and deal with pleasurable feelings they may have experienced, their need to feel "clean," or their need to assert power and dominance. Cases of homosexual assault may be even more confusing to children (p. 207).

Family-Centered Approaches to Helping Traumatized Children. Zilbach (1986) has consistently pointed out that children are often ignored in family therapy. This is particularly true when the presenting problem is most associated with the marital relationship and when the children are five years old or younger. But, she points out, even when the initial complaint is associated with an obvious childhood behavior pattern, family therapists have the tendency to assume that the problem is symptomatic of a dysfunctional family pattern. Quickly attention shifts to the parent-child or, most often, the marital relationship. A more recent version of her approaches (Zilbach, 1989) and those of others is available for additional reading.

Empowerment Approach to Helping Families Help Children

Although my experience in treating traumatized children is limited, compared to those whose work I have reviewed, I have found that parental and familial factors are often associated with childhood traumatic stress. Our approach, however, attends to the presenting childhood PTSD but does not assume major psychopathology with either the child or the family system within which the child resides.

My methods of helping children draw on the above literature and educate the families about childhood trauma and recovery. I have found that families attempting to cope with an extraordinarily stressful event, including those that affect children, for example, tend to want to draw together for mutual comfort and emotional assistance. Yet, at the same time, because family interaction under stressful conditions often increases stress, there is also a tendency to separate, to avoid interaction, particularly discussions of the trauma.

Children need to be involved in the process of helping families cope with and recover from their trauma. However, some children may not be ready to handle the tremendous tensions that evolve with the sessions. We have found that the following guidelines are useful in deciding when and how to involve children in our treatment approach.

Guidelines for Involving Children in Treatment. Perhaps the most direct way of presenting my approach in working with children would be to describe the set of guidelines I use. These guidelines are in the form of four general questions.

1. Is the child interested in being involved? Some children are unable to sustain their attention long enough in family sessions, particularly when the focus is not on them. However, if the child wants to be with her or his family, for one reason or another, it is important to allow the child to do so. By denying the child access to the sessions, we run the risk of generating additional traumatic experiences and requiring more time to recover.

Often children feel uncomfortable when the sessions exclusively focus on themselves. Younger children tend to cling to either or both parents and rarely agree to seeing the therapist alone. Older children feel that their parents are dumping them onto the therapist as punishment for not recovering faster from the traumatic event.

Our approach, as described earlier in this book, is to quickly shift attention away from the individual "victim" in the family and on the family system: how family *relationships* have changed as a result of the traumatic event and various methods of changing them back to suit the family members.

2. Is the child capable of comprehending the sessions? If the child is unable to take advantage of the discussions within

the session and to take an active part in them, it is better to provide productive activities for him or her within the session. Joan
Zilbach (1986, 1989) discusses a wide variety of in-session child
activities. These play activities are not designed to simply keep
the child preoccupied. They are useful in helping children identify and express their traumatic fears and views.

One method we have used frequently is to ask a child to
do us a favor during the session, for example, to produce a
series of drawings that represent how everyone in the family is
feeling now. After that we ask the child to describe the "thing"
that is causing these feelings. We interrupt the sessions when the
child is ready to report on her or his projects. In this way the
child has an important role, and her or his products or views can
be incorporated into the family's "healing theory."

*3. Are the child's traumatic experiences and reactions
being handled properly by the family?* Beyond working with
children within the session, it is important to observe how the
family deals with the children, particularly with regard to the
child's traumatic experiences. Some families may need some
coaching or parent education in order to help them care for the
child. Schaefer, Millman, Sichel, and Zwilling (1986) and
McMahon and R. DeV. Peters (1985) have assembled a fine collection of approaches in helping children with various difficulties, including stress disorders. A more popular book, *"So the
Witch Won't Eat Me"* by Dorothy Block (1978), might be suggested to some families.

In many ways families are more capable and experienced
in dealing with a traumatized child than with any other member—
perhaps because children are so vulnerable and are not shy about
asking for help. Most often we can sense the child's pain and
can react to it without hesitation. At the same time children are
excellent detectors of the mood and spirit of the family. Children
can often more quickly sense and describe what is happening in
the family, particularly when they are struggling with a traumatic experience.

*4. Should the child be excluded from any aspect of the
therapy?* I have found that if the child is an integral part of the
traumatic event and post-traumatic stress, she or he should be

an integral part of the treatment program. Just as at home, there are some *conversations* in which children should or should not be included, depending on the values and attitudes of the parents. At the same time it is important to be aware of the developmental differences between adults and children with regard to attention span, cognitive and verbal ability, and other factors affecting the productive use of therapy session time.

Conclusion

Children should be included in nearly all aspects of the therapy and recovery process. Some creativity is needed, of course, to ensure that their interest and unique talents are fully engaged.

It should be apparent by now that my empowering approach to helping traumatized children is not significantly different than that for helping adults. Most often the presenting problem is the symptoms or behaviors of the child. Parents want the child "helped" by eliminating these things and often assume that this can be done without their help or any substantial changes within the family system. As I have tried to illustrate in this chapter, helping traumatized children is both a means and an end in helping the entire family, shifting the focus from the child to the family.

Case of the Rose Family

Rather than return to the Murray family, perhaps another case will be more useful and interesting. The Rose family (dual-career parents in their thirties with a six-year-old son and a four-year-old daughter) were referred by their family physician, who believed that their daughter, Jennifer's, chronic headaches might be associated with the death of a family dog, Lady.

On the telephone and during the first session I was able to complete Phase I, establishing commitment to three specific goals of treatment: elimination of the headaches, development of parental skills in helping their children cope with traumatic events, and elimination of any residual grief associated with the death of Lady. Moreover, I was able to elicit the necessary information surrounding this problem from all family members. As it turned out, the entire family was still grieving over the death of Lady, which had occurred over a month earlier. In addition, there was some anxiety about the new school year (new schools for both the children due to graduation from either preschool or elementary school), which would begin next month, and about going on vacation in another week.

It became evident that Lady's death was handled differently by everyone. Only Jennifer had appeared very upset and been encouraged to forget about Lady as soon as possible.

I quickly voiced surprise at the family's ability to put Lady's death behind them, given how much they cared for her. I went on to give my assessment of the situation before specific goals were established.

Therapist: It appears that Jennifer has bravely assumed the role of family mourner for Lady. I am sure everyone appreciates this but would rather have Jennifer share this responsibility with her parents and brother. Next session, I would like to hold a memorial service for Lady, and I would like to plan the service with the rest of the time we have today.

Each family member made suggestions about what to do and to explain what Lady and her death meant to her or him. I attempted to urge the family members to talk to each other rather than through me, and I asked each to describe his or her own feelings as much as he or she could. Between sessions I had them think about Lady at least once a day together, preferably at the evening meal, and answer at least one question by the next session: "What would Lady want the family to do now that she is gone?"

The next session included a brief discussion of what had happened during the week. Jennifer's symptoms had disappeared. Everyone spoke openly of their love for Lady and their sadness about her dying. The ceremony was quite personal and moving. Most had tears in her or his eyes. Together the family had decided to buy a puppy that looked as much like Lady as possible and preferably was born or conceived at about the time Lady died. I asked them to each write a brief note to Lady between sessions telling her what they had done and what they planned to do. I also asked them to develop a plan for dealing with any future deaths.

The next and final session involved their sharing their notes and setting up a date in a month when I could call them. The purpose of the call would be to get a progress report on the puppy and any other news.

The family had developed a healing theory that emerged from the obvious pain and suffering of Jennifer and reflected the family's love and appreciation for their long-time family pet, the realization that it was too painful to openly talk about her death, and their appreciation that Jennifer had reminded them that they had unfinished business: mourning Lady's death. They agreed that it was a learning experience and that they would be more prepared for future deaths.

CHAPTER 12

Helping Traumatized Families: Challenges for Research and Practice

As therapists struggle to bring closure to a clinical case, authors struggle to bring closure to a book, particularly clinical authors. But just as the antidote for the former is to rely on one's objectives as an indicator of completion, so too must the objectives of a book, this book, provide direction for closure, an ending. I will first discuss the objectives with which I began this book and then turn to the implications of this work, as I see them today.

Goals and Objectives

From the beginning I have tried to share with you the theories, perspectives, basic assumptions, and methods I use for helping traumatized families. Specifically, I wanted to reach at least three separate objectives: (1) to review what we know about traumatized families, including definitions of some important concepts and several theoretical models that clarify these concepts; (2) to discuss the typical ways families cope with trauma, including both functional and dysfunctional patterns of coping; and (3) to describe a comprehensive approach to treating a variety of traumatized families.

I tried to focus the first chapter on the first objective. There I noted how and why I view families as systems and expanded on this view in the next several chapters by describing

139

the building blocks of my theory of processes of traumatized families. Also in the first chapter I defined what I meant by trauma and who I thought constituted "traumatized families." I went on in that chapter to emphasize the universality of trauma—how many more people, and thus families, are traumatized than we once thought.

Similarly, the second chapter included most of the material for addressing the second objective of the book. In the second chapter I noted how important families are and how they have natural and effective ways of helping traumatized members (detecting traumatic stress, urging confrontation of the stressor, urging recapitulation of the catastrophe, and facilitating resolution of the conflicts). I also reviewed the ways families are naturally supportive of one another. Indeed, they are so effective and efficient in helping traumatized members that I have tailored my empowerment treatment approach based on these naturally existing methods. They are first clarifying insights, correcting distortions, and supporting reframes.

However, just as families are so important in helping their members, they can also be a context for abuse precisely because of their unique role. Sometimes the abuse is inadvertent and covert. But in the case of family abuse, it is grossly intentional and overt with extraordinary emotional costs.

A way of summarizing the powerful role families play in human functioning and the process by which the family systems confront and recover from trauma is the family adaptation model presented in Chapter Two. It provided a context for appreciating the variety of ways families cope with a wide variety of stressors and clarified the characteristics that tend to differentiate functional and dysfunctional family coping, which were described at the end of the chapter.

The other chapters addressed the third objective of the book. Chapter Three presented the theoretical building blocks for my approach to conceptualizing, assessing, and treating traumatized families. Here I noted that I attempt to *empower the family to make peace with the past and take charge of their lives;* that this kind of intervention could be categorized as primary prevention, as well as secondary prevention. In addition to helping families make peace with the past, I try to educate them about trauma, traumatic stress, family functioning, and recovery. Moreover, I attempt to enhance their natural resources, including their basic family social skills and supportiveness.

The other chapters included a detailed description of the treatment preconditions of my intervention, my methods of assessment, and, beginning with Chapter Five, a detailed description of my five-phase approach to empowering traumatized families, including children.

The Traumatizing Family

Approaches to helping traumatized families emerge from a wide variety of scientific inquiries about families who do not ordinarily seek treatment. Indeed, the clinical literature, by focusing on psychopathology and dysfunction, frequently represents families—either implicitly or explicitly—as the cause of mental illness. Recent monographs (see Pilisuk & Parks, 1986), however, challenge this view and suggest that families, in particular, and social support networks and groups, in general, provide a vital and often overlooked function in fostering mental health and well-being.

My approach to helping traumatized families assumes that the family was functioning acceptably well for all its members prior to the impact of the traumatic event. Moreover, victimized family members may find more effective emotional support from sources other than the family. Even well-intentioned families can be enormously ineffective in helping some family members, for a variety of reasons. But in spite of these obvious limitations of utilizing or empowering families to help each other, I believe it is the method of choice for most of them.

By intervening at the family systems level, my many colleagues and I believe that not only will the pain and suffering of members be alleviated but also, as a result of the intervention, the family will be more equipped to cope effectively with future challenges. This assertion, too, should be tested.

Toward a Field of Traumatic Stress. In the premiere issue of the *Journal of Traumatic Stress* I suggested (Figley, 1988c) that there was sufficient evidence to declare that a new field, traumatic stress studies, existed. Perhaps the most understudied area in this new field is the immediate and long-term *systemic* consequences of highly stressful events and the most effective methods of measuring and treating these traumatized systems. This is one of the reasons why I wrote this book—to attempt to begin to fill that need.

Indeed, with the considerable growth of the field of traumatic stress (Figley, 1988d), it is probably only a matter of time before important research studies will address the many unanswered questions. What is critical, however, are new studies of non-help-seeking people who have been exposed to traumatic events (Quarantelli, 1985).

From these studies we may begin to establish accurate estimates of the full human impact of highly stressful events, beyond the current estimates that include only those directly involved, the "victims" (Figley, 1985b). Among them we may find the hidden victims of traumatic events. What are the major differences between those who recover from potentially traumatic events and those who do not? What accounts for the speed and fact of recovery? Do the family and social support system play a role, or is recovery a result of some other factor or set of factors, some of which have yet to be detected?

Research Challenges

Obviously, my approach to helping traumatized families is based on numerous assumptions that need to be tested and verified or changed. The major assumption of this approach to post-traumatic family therapy, for example, is that treatment should, at the very least, focus on the social supportive function of the family system and attempt to restore it at least to pre-trauma levels. This assumption should of course be tested under rigorous scientific conditions in order to be supported or refuted.

My family empowerment approach certainly should be tested and contrasted with others that also purport to be effective in helping traumatized families. Assuming that this approach is useful and appropriate, what are the implications for future research and treatment innovation? Certainly, traumatic events and the associated stress of individuals and social systems have always existed. Most recently, traumatic stress studies have made significant strides in identifying the major parameters that account for why people are traumatized and the process by which they recover. Moreover, the social support systems and the family in particular are extremely important resources in the recovery process. Comprehensive and effective intervention programs to prevent and treat traumatic stress must include some form of family treatment.

Beyond outcome studies, however, it is important to verify the findings of Kishur (1984), who found evidence of the chiasmal effect of the "transfer" of traumatic symptoms to supporters. It is important to include this in future studies of the incidence and prevalence of PTSD among various groups of victims and evaluation of the victims' closest supporters.

Clinical Challenges

As I have tried to demonstrate throughout this book, the effective and efficient treatment of traumatized families requires careful attention to many factors. One of the most important factors is the client's access to an effective social support system (Burge & Figley, 1987). For example, those who are separated from family and friends and lack the social skills to establish and maintain close interpersonal relationships are more vulnerable to traumatic stress. In contrast, those who enjoy an active and vibrant social life are able to avoid and quickly overcome troubling life events. Perhaps the most critical roles psychotherapists and other professional helpers play is that of social supporter. Are there other ways of providing such support than in clinical settings?

For those clients who *do* have access to social support, particularly intact systems such as a family, the system itself may require mental health services. Just as family therapy emerged as a result of clinicians' struggling with efforts to cure individuals with major mental illness, family therapy might be the treatment of choice for the traumatized.

The field of family therapy is quickly becoming one of

the most powerful and promising in psychotherapy. Although few have discussed the utility of family therapy in traumatic stress treatment, I hope that this book has illustrated the role of family therapy in treating not only the victims but also the co-victims, fellow family members, and the family system within which they reside. By selecting the *family as the unit of intervention*, we are assured not only of ameliorating the unwanted side effects of traumatic stress but also of equipping the family to cope more effectively with any future adversities.

Personal Challenges: Avoiding Burnout

I entered the fields of family therapy and traumatic stress following graduate school in 1974. I have never regretted it. I believe that this is true for a majority of my colleagues who have treated families. There is considerable pleasure in knowing that you have made a significant contribution to the recovery of individuals and families struggling to overcome hardship.

Sadly, however, I have seen many colleagues and friends abandon clinical work because of their inability to cope with the troubles of others. This is particularly true for those who work with "victims" of various catastrophes. For those of you who choose to help the traumatized family, the challenges will be even greater, because working with families is much more encompassing than working with individuals. Couples and families have a remarkable ability to draw the therapist into their system, although most therapists resist this membership and attempt to remain unaligned, positioning themselves with various alliances for strategic reasons. However, the effort to remain aligned takes enormous concentration.

Moreover, the same kind of psychosocial mechanisms within families that make trauma "contagious," that create a context for family members to infect one another with their traumatic material, operate between traumatized clients and the therapist.

Those therapists most at risk to abandon their proper role, however, are those who begin to *view themselves as saviors, or at least as rescuers*. Some of these clinical "rescuers" have the resources and skills to avoid having this role intrude in their life, becoming addictive or at least succumbing to countertransference. These can be particularly problematical in working with traumatized families.

Not long ago NiCarthy, Merriam, and Coffman (1984) urged those who work with abused women to become familiar with the stages and signs of burnout in working with this population. The same kinds of warnings can be applied to working with other types of traumatized populations. Among the symptoms they cite are emotional and physical exhaustion that includes but is not limited to headaches, muscle tension, depression, boredom, apathy, absenteeism, decline in performance, hypertension, insomnia, irritability, increased anxiety, increased smoking, drinking, drug dependency, other addictions, dysfunctional escape activities (overeating, daydreaming), stress-related physical and emotional ailments, tension with family and/or friends, self-doubt and blame, and general disillusionment.

Help for the Helpers. There are ways of overcoming these problems. Among the many methods of both avoiding and eliminating the "savior syndrome," NiCathy et al. (1984) and others (Cherniss, 1980; Edelwich & Brodsky, 1980; Pines, Aronson, & Kafray, 1981; Figley, 1982, 1985b; Maslach, 1982; Rando, 1984) suggest the following.

    1. Comprehensive education about stress and coping. I have urged for many years (see, for example, Figley & McCubbin, 1983) that professional training in the helping professions generally includes courses and in-service training programs that focus on normative and catastrophic stressors. These programs should identify not only the common methods that individuals, families, and other systems use in reaction to stress but also the stressors that are unique to the helping professions, particularly the pitfalls in working with traumatized clients.

    2. Developing and maintaining membership in supportive networks. Therapists often cannot help but bring home their work. This is particularly true if the thoughts and feelings associated with clients involuntarily intrude on their personal life. Often it requires another professional who has experienced these symptoms to truly understand and provide emotional support. It is appropriate, therefore, to reserve sufficient time at the end of a case conference or professional meeting for some personal processing. It would be an opportunity to share the emotional burdens of clinical work without shame or indignity. Group members can provide not only emotional support and encouragement, ingredients that are vital to the maintenance of good mental health. They can also serve as role models, sources of information and ideas about methods of coping.

3. Self-care and pleasure. The joy of our own lives is sometimes lost when we focus on the joylessness of the lives of our clients. Some of us may even feel guilty for feeling contentment and satisfaction with ourselves and our families. Yet our own life satisfaction makes us more adept at helping others find such satisfaction. Cultivating interesting hobbies, enjoying vacations, recreational activities, and time with family and friends are good not only for us but also for our clients.

4. Setting realistic goals, limits, and boundaries. Finally, I have learned over the years that I have just so much time, energy, interest, and sensitivity. I have learned to distribute these finite resources according to my values and to be constantly vigilant about overdistribution. Otherwise, I have an insufficient amount of time, energy, interest, and sensitivity for my family, friends, and myself. I have suffered a great deal at times when I was *not vigilant enough* and sacrificed these personal resources for other things (such as career and clients).

My worst experiences with clients—traumatized or not— were those who wanted more than I could give. My salvation was the realization that I had done as much as I could at the time and that I could help the client and another helper begin where I left off.

I recall when I completed my first book, *Stress Disorders Among Vietnam Veterans: Theory, Research, and Treatment* (Figley, 1978). I felt an extraordinary sense of relief. The relief came from believing that I had made a contribution, not just to the mental health field but also to helping a group of men and women who were not as lucky as I and whom I wished very much to help.

I wish you well in your work with traumatized families. I have tried to share with you what I have done, the mistakes as well as the successes. I hope that you will write and tell me of yours. Good luck.

RESOURCE A

Traumagram Questionnaire

Part A: Identifying the Stressor and Recovery Dates

1. Use the space below to identify all of the major events in your life that were extraordinarily stressful, either at the time or since then—for example, those that left lingering, troubling memories for a time. Also please estimate how long both the stressor event lasted and when and how long was your recovery. An example might be as follows:

Stressor Event	Date of Event	Dates of Recovery
A: Auto accident as teen	12/59	12/59–3/60, 12/60–1/61, 3/63–4/63
B: Death of maternal grandfather	3/67	3/67–7/67, 3/68, 7/70, 9/82

[These first two entries indicate that the client experienced two highly stressful and memorable events. Event A happened in December of 1959, and the client experienced three periods of readjustment. Similarly, Event B happened in March of 1967 with four periods of readjustment.]

| | Date of | Dates of |
| Stressor Event | Event | Recovery |

A : _____
B : _____
C : _____
D : _____
E : _____

Part B: Circumstances of the Stressor

Please consider the above stressors in the questions below. If you experienced more than 5 stressors, please complete additional questionnaires until all are described.

2. Regarding *Stressor A*, please list the names of at least one other person who also experienced this stressor.

| *Name* | *Age at Time* | *Relationship to You* |

_____

_____

3. Regarding *Stressor B*, please list the names of at least one other person who also experienced this stressor.

| *Name* | *Age at Time* | *Relationship to You* |

_____

_____

4. Regarding *Stressor C*, please list the names of at least one other person who also experienced this stressor.

| *Name* | *Age at Time* | *Relationship to You* |

_____

_____

5. Regarding *Stressor D*, please list the names of at least one other person who also experienced this stressor.

    Name   *Age at Time*   *Relationship to You*

_____

_____

6. Regarding *Stressor E*, please list the names of at least one other person who also experienced this stressor.

    Name   *Age at Time*   *Relationship to You*

_____

_____

Part C: Estimating the Stress and Coping Factors of Each Stressor

7. Please indicate the degree of stress you experienced as a direct result of the stressors noted above.

Stressor															
	At the Time					A Year Later					Now				
	High	Mdn	Low			High	Mdn	Low			High	Mdn	Low		
A	5	4	3	2	1	5	4	3	2	1	5	4	3	2	1
B	5	4	3	2	1	5	4	3	2	1	5	4	3	2	1
C	5	4	3	2	1	5	4	3	2	1	5	4	3	2	1
D	5	4	3	2	1	5	4	3	2	1	5	4	3	2	1
E	5	4	3	2	1	5	4	3	2	1	5	4	3	2	1

Degree of Stressfulness

8. Please consider each traumatic experience and indicate briefly what helped or hindered your coping with the stressor.

Stressor A: _____

_____

Stressor B: _____

_____

Stressor C: _____

Stressor D: _____

Stressor E: _____

9. Overall, what do you believe are the common features that account for your adjusting or not adjusting to traumatic events in your life? _____

_____

_____

Source: © Charles R. Figley, 1987.

The Purdue Post-Traumatic Stress Disorder Scale

These questions ask about your reactions to an event in your life. The event in your life to use as a basis for your answers is _____

_____.

The first eleven questions ask about your reactions during the *past seven days.* The last four questions ask about your reactions since the event happened. *Circle one number for each question.*

During the past seven days, including today . . .

		Not At All	Moder- ately	Ex- tremely
1.	How much have you been bothered by memories or thoughts of the event when you didn't want to think about it?	1	2	3	4
2.	How often have you dreamed about the event?	1	2	3	4
3.	How often have you suddenly felt as if you were experiencing the event again?	1	2	3	4

		Not At All	*Moder- ately*	*Ex- tremely*	
4.	How much have you felt un-usually distant or detached from people?	1	2	3	4
5.	To what extent have you felt that you just couldn't respond to things emotionally the way you used to?	1	2	3	4
6.	How much have you found yourself extra alert to possible danger?	1	2	3	4
7.	To what extent are you more jumpy than usual?	1	2	3	4
8.	To what extent have you had more trouble sleeping than usual?	1	2	3	4
9.	How often have you had more trouble than usual remember-ing things or concentrating?	1	2	3	4
10.	To what extent have you avoided activities that re-minded you of the event?	1	2	3	4
11.	How much do the reactions de-scribed in items 1–10 get worse when you've been in situations that remind you of the event?	1	2	3	4

Since the event happened . . .

		Not At All	*Moder- ately*	*Ex- tremely*	
12.	To what extent have you lost interest in one or more of your usual activities (e.g., work, hobbies, exercise, sports, entertainment, church)?	1	2	3	4
13.	To what extent have you felt guilty about surviving or about what you had to do to survive during the event?	1	2	3	4

		Not At All	Moder- ately	Ex- tremely
14.	How much has this event distressed or upset you?	1	2 3	4
15.	How much do you think this event would upset or distress most people?	1	2 3	4

The Purdue
Social Support Scale

I am interested in knowing where people go when they need social support. Please answer the following questions as well as you can. Answer all questions in each section before moving on.

PART I:

Do not feel that you must fill all of the blanks below, but use as many as you want.

1. In times of need, people generally turn to others for help. In the spaces below, please list those people (first names only) that you would turn to.

2. Next to each name, please indicate each person's relationship to you—for example, is he/she a friend, neighbor, spouse, parent, uncle, pastor, physician?

See the example for filling out Part I.

Note: This protected scale was developed by Sandra Burge and Charles R. Figley. It is available from the second author at the Family Research Institute, 525 Russell Street, Purdue University, West Lafayette, Ind. 47906.

Example for filling out PART I

NAME OF PERSON(S)/RELATIONSHIP		NAME OF PERSON(S)/RELATIONSHIP	
Geni	Mom		
Bill	Friend		
Julie	Sister		
Dr. Gold	Therapist		

PART II:

Below are 6 columns representing different ways in which people may be helpful. They are:

(a) EMOTIONAL SUPPORT . . . . referring to care, comfort, love, affection, sympathy, being on your side

(b) ENCOURAGEMENT . . . . referring to being encouraging, praising or complimenting you, making you feel important

(c) ADVICE . . . . referring to advice as well as providing useful information and help with solving problems

(d) COMPANIONSHIP . . . . referring to spending time together, doing things together, visiting each other

(e) TANGIBLE AID . . . . referring to helping with chores or projects, baby-sitting, transportation, and/or lending money when needed

(f) OVERALL HELPFULNESS . . referring to being generally helpful when needed

3. Now I am interested in knowing how satisfied you would expect to be with the support that these people may provide. In the boxes below, consider each person in the previous list according to the six characteristics defined above and rate your EXPECTED SATISFACTION with each person's help.

Use this scale to rate your satisfaction:

"4" means Very Satisfied
"3" means Satisfied
"2" means Dissatisfied
"1" means Very Dissatisfied
"0" means Wouldn't Seek This

Please fill all 6 columns for each person listed using the above scale.

EMOTIONAL SUPPORT	ENCOURAGE-MENT	ADVICE	COMPANION-SHIP	TANGIBLE AID	OVERALL HELPFULNESS

REFERENCES

American Psychiatric Association (1980). *Diagnostic and statistical manual of mental disorders* (3rd. ed.). Washington, D.C.: Author.

American Psychiatric Association (1987). *Diagnostic and statistical manual of mental disorders* (rev. 3rd. ed.). Washington, D.C.: Author.

Berecz, J. M. (1968). Phobias of childhood: Etiology and treatment. *Psychological Bulletin, 70*(6), 694–720.

Block, D. (1978). *"So the witch won't eat me": Fantasy and the child's fear of infanticide.* New York: Grove Press.

Bowlby, J. (1961). Processes of mourning. *International Journal of Psychoanalysis, 44,* 317.

Bowlby, J. (1969). *Attachment and loss, vol. 1.* New York: Basic Books.

Bowlby, J. (1980). *Attachment and loss, vol. 3: Loss, sadness, and depression.* New York: Basic Books.

Brownell, A., & Shumaker, S. A. (1984). Social support: An introduction to a complex phenomenon. *Journal of Social Issues, 4,* 1–9.

Burge, S. K., & Figley, C. R. (1987). The social support scale: Development and initial estimates of reliability and validity. *Victimology, 12*(1), 14–22.

Burgess, A. W., & Holmstron, L. L. (1979). *Rape: Crisis and recovery.* Bowie, Md.: Brady.

Cannon, W. B. (1939). *The wisdom of the body.* New York: Morton.

Caplan, G. (1964). *Principles of preventive psychiatry.* New York: Basic Books.

Caplan, G. (1974). *Support systems and community mental health.* New York: Behavioral Publications.

Cherniss, C. (1980). *Staff burnout: Job stress in the human services.* Newbury Park, Calif.: Sage.

Cohen, S., Komermarck, J., & Mermelstein, R. (1983). Global measure of perceived stress. *Journal of Health and Social Behavior, 24,* 385–396.

Derogatis, L. R. (1977). *The SCL–90R: Administration, scoring and procedures manual-I.* Baltimore: Clinical Psychometric Research.

Derogatis, L. R., & Spencer, P. M. (1982). *The brief symptom inventory (BSI): Administration, scoring and procedures manual-I.* Baltimore: Johns Hopkins University.

Edelwich, J., & Brodsky, A. (1980). *Burn-out: Stages of disillusionment in the helping professions.* New York: Human Sciences Press.

Eitinger, L. (1982). The effects of captivity. In F. M. Ochberg & D. A. Soskis (Eds.), *Victims of terrorism* (pp. 73–94). Boulder, Colorado: Westview.

Erickson, C. A. (1989). Rape and the family. In C. R. Figley (Ed.), *Treating stress in families* (pp. 257–290). New York: Brunner/Mazel.

Eth, S., & Pynoos, R. S. (1985a). Developmental perspectives on psychic trauma. In C. R. Figley (Ed.), *Trauma and its wake: The study and treatment of post-traumatic stress disorder* (pp. 36–52). New York: Brunner/Mazel.

Eth, S., & Pynoos, R. S. (Eds.). (1985b). *Post-traumatic stress disorder in children.* Washington, D.C.: American Psychiatric Press.

Farmer, R. E., Monahan, L. H., & Hekeler, R. W. (1984). *Stress management for human services.* Newbury Park, Calif.: Sage.

Figley, C. R. (1973). Child density and the marital relationship. *Journal of Marriage and the Family, 45*(3), 211–223.

Figley, C. R. (1975a, February 19). Interpersonal adjustment and family life among Vietnam veterans, a general bibliography. *Congressional Record* (Entered by Senator Hartke).

Figley, C. R. (1975b, August). *Contrasts between combat and noncombat Vietnam veterans regarding selected indices of interpersonal adjustment.* Paper presented at the annual meeting of the American Sociological Association, San Francisco.

Figley, C. R. (1975c, August). *The returning veteran and interpersonal adjustment: A review of the research.* Paper presented at the annual meeting of the National Council on Family Relations, Salt Lake City.

Figley, C. R. (1976a, October). *Combat-related stress disorders: Family therapy implications.* Paper presented at the annual meeting of the American Association of Marriage and Family Counselors, Philadelphia.

Figley, C. R. (1976b, September). *An overview of the research related to delayed combat stress among Vietnam veterans.* Paper presented at the annual meeting of the American Psychological Association, Washington, D.C.

Figley, C. R. (1978). Psychosocial adjustment among Vietnam veterans: An overview of the research. In C. R. Figley (Ed.), *Stress disorders among Vietnam veterans: Theory, research, and treatment* (pp. 57–70). New York: Brunner/Mazel.

Figley, C. R. (1979). *Combat as disaster: Treating combat veterans as survivors.* Invited address to the American Psychiatric Association, Chicago.

Figley, C. R. (1980, February). *The algorithmic approach to treating post-traumatic stress reactions.* Presented at a Clinical Workshop on Treating Combat-Related Stress Disorders. Veterans Administration Regional Medical Education Center, St. Louis.

Figley, C. R. (1982, January). *Traumatization and comfort: Close relationships may be hazardous to your health.* Invited lecture, Texas Tech University, Lubbock, Texas.

Figley, C. R. (1983) Catastrophes: An overview of family reactions. In C. R. Figley & H. I. McCubbin (Eds.), *Stress and the family: Vol. 2. Coping with catastrophe* (pp. 3–20). New York: Brunner/Mazel.

Figley, C. R. (1984). Treating post-traumatic stress disorder:

The algorithmic approach. *American Academy of Psychiatry and the Law Newsletter, 9*(3), 7–9.

Figley, C. R. (1985a). The family as victim: Mental health implications. *Psychiatry, 6,* 283–291.

Figley, C. R. (1985b). From victim to survivor: Social responsibility in the wake of catastrophe. In C. R. Figley (Ed.), *Trauma and its wake: The study and treatment of post-traumatic stress disorder* (pp. 398–416). New York: Brunner/Mazel.

Figley, C. R. (1985c). Introduction. In C. R. Figley (Ed.), *Trauma and its wake: The study and treatment of post-traumatic stress disorder* (pp. xvii–xxvi). New York: Brunner/Mazel.

Figley, C. R. (1986a, June). *Family traumatic stress.* Invited presentation at the annual meeting of the American Family Therapy Association, Washington, D.C.

Figley, C. R. (1986b). Introduction. In C. R. Figley (Ed.), *Trauma and its wake: Vol. 2. Post-traumatic stress disorder: Theory, research, and treatment* (pp. xvii–xxix). New York: Brunner/Mazel.

Figley, C. R. (1986c). Post-traumatic stress: The role of the family. *Emotional First Aid: Journal of Crisis Intervention,* Fall, 58–70.

Figley, C. R. (1986d). Traumatic stress: The role of the family and social support systems. In C. R. Figley (Ed.), *Trauma and its wake: Vol. 2. Post-traumatic stress disorder: Theory, research, and treatment* (pp. 39–56). New York: Brunner/Mazel.

Figley, C. R. (1988a). A five-phase treatment of family traumatic stress. *Journal of Traumatic Stress, 1*(1), 127–141.

Figley, C. R. (1988b). *Helping traumatized families: Recent innovations.* Invited keynote address at the annual conference of the Society for Traumatic Stress Studies, Dallas.

Figley, C. R. (1988c). Post-traumatic family therapy. In F. Ochberg (Ed.), *Post-traumatic therapy* (pp. 83–110). New York: Brunner/Mazel.

Figley, C. R. (1988d). Toward a field of traumatic stress studies. *Journal of Traumatic Stress, 1*(1), 3–11.

Figley, C. R., & McCubbin, H. I. (1983). Looking to the future: Research, education, treatment, and policy. In C. R. Figley &

H. I. McCubbin (Eds.), *Stress and the family: Vol. 2. Coping with catastrophe* (pp. 185–196). New York: Brunner/Mazel.

Figley, C. R., & Sprenkle, D. H. (1978). Delayed stress response syndrome: Family therapy indications. *Journal of Marriage and Family Counseling, 4,* 53–60.

Fisch, R., Weakland, J. H., & Segal, L. (1982). *The tactics of change: Doing therapy briefly.* San Francisco: Jossey-Bass.

Fraser, J. S. (1989). The strategic rapid intervention approach. In C. R. Figley (Ed.), *Treating stress in families* (pp. 122–157). New York: Brunner/Mazel.

Gleser, G., Green, B. L., & Winget, C. (1981). *Prolonged psychosocial effects of disaster: A study of Buffalo Creek.* New York: Academic Press.

Gottlieb, B. H. (Ed.). (1983). *Social support strategies: Guidelines for mental health practice.* Newbury Park, Calif.: Sage.

Gottlieb, B. H. (Ed.). (1988). *Marshaling social support: Formats, processes, and effects.* Newbury Park, Calif.: Sage.

Green, A. H. (1978). Psychiatric treatment of abused children. *Journal of the American Academy of Child Psychiatry, 17,* 356–371.

Green, B. L., Wilson, J. P., & Lindy, J. (1985). Conceptualizing post-traumatic stress disorder: A psychosocial framework. In C. R. Figley (Ed.), *Trauma and its wake: The study and treatment of post-traumatic stress disorder* (pp. 53–72). New York: Brunner/Mazel.

Guerney, B. G. (1977). *Relationship enhancement: Skill-training programs for therapy, problem prevention, and enrichment.* San Francisco: Jossey-Bass.

Guerney, B. G. (1982). Relationship enhancement. In E. K. Marshall & P. D. Kurtz (Eds.), *Interpersonal Helping Skills* (pp. 482–518). San Francisco: Jossey-Bass.

Guerney, B. G., Jr., Guerney, L. F., & Cooney, T. M. (1985). Marital and family problem prevention and enrichment programs. In L. L'Abate (Ed.), *Handbook of family psychology.* Homewood, Ill.: Dow-Jones Irwin.

Haley, J. (1973). *Uncommon therapy.* New York: Norton.

Haley, J. (1976). *Problem-solving therapy.* San Francisco: Jossey-Bass.

Haley, J. (1984). *Ordeal therapy: Unusual ways to change behavior.* San Francisco: Jossey-Bass.

Harris, C. J. (1988). *Learned helplessness attributional style as a predictor of and a precursor to post-traumatic stress disorder: Individual and family considerations.* Ph.D. dissertation, Purdue University.

Hartsough, D. (1988). A screening scale for estimating post-traumatic stress disorder. The Purdue PTSD Scale. Purdue University, West Lafayette, Indiana.

Herman, J. (1981). *Father-daughter incest.* Cambridge, Mass.: Harvard University Press.

Herrington, L. H. (1985). Victims of crime: Their plight, our response. *American Psychologist, 40*(1), 99–103.

Hetherington, E. M., Cox, M., and Cox, R. (1976). Divorced fathers. *The Family Coordinator, 25,* 417–428.

Hill, R. (1949). *Families under stress.* New York: Harper & Row.

Hill, R., & Hansen, D. (1965). The family in disaster. In G. Baker & D. S. Chapman (Eds.), *Man and society in disaster* (pp. 37–51). New York: Basic Books.

Horowitz, M. J. (1986). *Stress response syndromes* (2nd ed.). Northvale, N.J.: Jason Aronson.

Horowitz, M., Wilner, N., Kaltreider, N., & Alvarez, W. (1980). Signs and symptoms of post-traumatic stress disorder. *Archives of General Psychiatry, 37,* 85–92.

Hyman, I. A., Zelikoff, W., & Clarke, J. (1987, September). *Understanding PTSD in children: A study of educator-induced trauma.* Unpublished paper presented at the annual meeting of the American Psychological Association, New York City.

Jacobson, G., Strickler, M., & Morley, W. (1968). Generic and individual approaches to crisis intervention. *American Journal of Public Health, 58,* 338–343.

Kanner, A., Coyne, J., Schaefer, C., & Lazarus, R. (1981). Comparison of two models of stress measurement: Daily hassles and uplifts versus major life events. *Journal of Behavioral Medicine, 4,* 1–37.

Kazdin, A. E., & Wilcoxin, L. A. (1976). Systemic desensitization and nonspecific treatment effects: A methodological evaluation. *Psychological Bulletin, 83,* 729–758.

Kishur, G. R. (1984). Chiasmal effects of traumatic stressors: The emotional costs of support. Masters thesis, Purdue University, West Lafayette, Indiana.

Kishur, G. R., & Figley, C. R. (1987). *The relationship between psychiatric symptoms of crime victims and their supporters: Evidence of the chiasmal effects of co-victimization.* Unpublished manuscript, Purdue University, West Lafayette, Indiana.

Kluft, R. P. (1984). Treatment of multiple personality in childhood. *Psychiatric Clinics of North America, 4,* 9–29.

Koss, M. P., Gidycz, C. A., & Wisniewski, P. (1987). The scope of rape: Incidence and prevalence of sexual aggression and victimization in a national sample of higher education students. *Journal of Consulting and Clinical Psychology, 55*(2), 162–170.

Levis, D. J., & Hare, N. A. (1977). A review of the theoretical rationale and empirical support for the extinction approach of implosive (flooding) therapy. In M. Hersen, R. M. Eisler, & P. M. Miller (Eds.), *Progress in behavior modification, Vol. 4.* New York: Academic Press.

Lindemann, E. (1944). Symptomatology and management of acute grief. *American Journal of Psychiatry, 101,* 141–148.

McCubbin, H., & Figley, C. R. (1983a). Bridging normative and catastrophic family stress. In H. I. McCubbin & C. R. Figley (Eds.), *Stress and the family: Vol. 1. Coping with normative transitions* (pp. xix–xxvi). New York: Brunner/Mazel.

McCubbin, H., & Figley, C. R. (1983b). Introduction. In H. I. McCubbin & C. R. Figley (Eds.), *Stress and the family: Vol. 1. Coping with normative transitions* (pp. xxi–xxxi). New York: Brunner/Mazel.

McCubbin, H. I., Joy, C., Cauble, E., Comeau, J., Patterson, J., & Needle, R. (1980). Family stress and coping: A decade review. *Journal of Marriage and the Family, 43*(4), 855–872.

McCubbin, H. I., & Patterson, J. (1983). Family transitions: Adaptation to stress. In H. I. McCubbin & C. R. Figley (Eds.), *Stress and the family: Vol. 1. Coping with normative transitions* (pp. 5–25). New York: Brunner/Mazel.

McMahon, R. J., & Peters, R. DeV. (Eds.). (1985). *Childhood disorders: Behavioral-developmental approaches.* New York: Brunner/Mazel.

Madanes, C. (1984). *Behind the one-way mirror: Advances in the practice of strategic therapy.* San Francisco: Jossey-Bass.

Mann, P. (1972). Residential mobility as an adaptive experience. *Journal of Consulting and Clinical Psychology, 39,* 37–42.

Maslach, C. (1982). *Burnout: The cost of caring.* Englewood Cliffs, N.J.: Prentice-Hall.

Miller, S., Nunnally, E. W., & Wackman, D. B. (1975). *Alive and aware: Improving communication in relationships.* Minneapolis: Interpersonal Communication Programs.

Mineka, S. (1979). The role of fear in theories of avoidance learning, flooding and extinction. *Psychological Bulletin, 86,* 985–1010.

Montgomery, B. (1982). *Family crisis as process: Persistence and change.* Washington, D.C.: University Press of America.

Mowbray, C. T. (1988). Post-traumatic therapy for children who are victims of violence. In F. M. Ochberg (Ed.), *Post-traumatic therapy and victims of violence* (pp. 196–212). New York: Brunner/Mazel.

Mowrer, O. H. (1947). On the dual nature of learning: A reinterpretation of "conditioning" and "problem solving." *Harvard Educational Review, 17,* 102–148.

Mowrer, O. H. (1960). *Learning theory and behavior.* New York: Wiley.

Murphy, L. B., & Moriarty, A. E. (1976). *Vulnerability, coping, and growth: From infancy to adolescence.* New Haven: Yale University Press.

NiCarthy, G., Merriam, K., & Coffman, S. (1984). *Talking it out: A guide to groups for abused women.* Seattle: Seal Press.

Ochberg, F. (Ed.). (1988). *Post-traumatic therapy.* New York: Brunner/Mazel.

Olson, D. H., McCubbin, H. I., Barnes, H., Larsen, A., Muxen, M., & Wilson, M. (1983). *Families: What makes them work.* Newbury Park, Calif.: Sage.

Olson, D. H., Russell, C. S., & Sprenkle, D. H. (1983). Circumplex model VI: Theoretical update. *Family Process, 22,* 69–83.

Olson, D. H., Russell, C. S., & Sprenkle, D. H. (Ed.). (1989). *Circumplex model: systemic assessment and treatment of families.* New York: Haworth.

Olson, D. H., Sprenkle, D. H., & Russell, C. S. (1979). Circumplex model of marital and family systems I: Cohesion and adaptability dimensions, family types, and clinical application. *Family Process, 18*, 3–28.

Osterweis, M., & Townsend, J. (1988). *Helping bereaved children: A booklet for school personnel.* DHHS Publication No. ADM 88-1553.

Parks, C. M. (1964). The effects of bereavement on physical and mental health: A study of the case records of widows. *British Medical Journal, 2,* 274.

Parks, C. M. (1972). Accuracy of predictions of survival in later stages of cancer. *British Medical Journal, 1,* 29–31.

Pilisuk, M., & Parks, S. H. (1986). *The healing web: Social networks and human survival.* Hanover, N.H.: University Press of New England.

Pines, A. M., Aronson, E., & Kafray, D. (1981). *Burnout: From tedium to personal growth.* New York: Free Press.

Procidano, M. S., & Heller, K. (1983). Measures of perceived social support from friends and family: Three validation studies. *American Journal of Community Psychiatry, 11,* 1–23.

Quarantelli, E. L. (1985). An assessment of conflicting views on mental health: The consequences of traumatic events. In C. R. Figley (Ed.), *Trauma and its wake: The study and treatment of post-treatment stress disorder* (pp. 173–218). New York: Brunner/Mazel.

Rabkin, J. G., & Struening, E. L. (1976). Life events, stress, and illness. *Science, 194,* 1013–1020.

Rahe, R. (1974). The pathway between subjects' recent life changes and their near future illness reports: Representative results and methodological issues. In B. P. Dohrenwend and B. S. Dohrenwend (Eds.), *Stressful life events: Their nature and effects.* New York: Wiley.

Rando, T. A. (1984). *Grief, dying, and death: Clinical interventions for caregivers.* Champaign, Ill.: Research Press.

Raphael, B. (1973). Bereavement: A paradigm for preventive medicine. *Sandoz Therapeutic Quarterly, 2,* 1–9.

Raphael, B. (1975). Crisis and loss: Counseling following a disaster. *Mental Health in Australia, 1*(4), 118–122.

Raphael, B. (1983). *The anatomy of bereavement.* New York: Basic Books.

Rimm, D. C., & Masters, J. C. (1979). *Behavior therapy: Techniques and empirical findings* (2nd. ed.). New York: Academic Press.

Rohrbaugh, M., Tennen, H., Press, S., White, L., Raskin, P., & Pickering, M. (1977). *Paradoxical strategies in psychotherapy.* Paper presented at the American Psychological Association, San Francisco.

Russell, C. S., & Olson, D. H. (1983). Circumplex model of marital and family systems: Review of empirical support and elaboration of therapeutic process. In D. A. Bagarozzi, A. P. Jurich, & R. W. Jackson (Eds.), *Marital and family therapy: New perspectives in theory, research and practice* (pp. 25–47). New York: Human Sciences Press.

Russell, D.E.H. (1984). *Sexual exploitation: Rape, child sexual abuse, and workplace harassment.* Newbury Park, Calif.: Sage.

Russell, D.E.H. (1986). *The secret trauma: Incest in the lives of girls and women.* New York: Basic Books.

Schaefer, C. E., Millman, H. L., Sichel, S. M., & Zwilling, J. R. (1986). *Advances in therapies for children.* San Francisco: Jossey-Bass.

Schlenger, W. E., Kulka, R. A., Fairbank, J. A., Hough, R. L., Jordan, B. K., Marmar, C. R., and Weiss, D. S. (in press). The prevalence of post-traumatic stress disorder in the Vietnam generation: Findings from the national Vietnam veterans readjustment study. *The New England Journal of Medicine.*

Segal, S. A. (1986). *The development of measures to assess traumatic appraisal.* Dissertation, Purdue University, West Lafayette, Indiana.

Segal, S. A., & Figley, C. R. (1988). The prevalence of highly stressful events in a college population, a letter to the editor. *Hospital and Community Psychiatry, 39*(9), 998.

Selye, H. (1956). *Stress in life.* New York: McGraw-Hill.

Selye, H. (1974). *Stress without distress.* New York: Lippincott.

Shumaker, S. A., & Brownell, A. (1985). Introduction: Social support intervention. *Journal of Social Issues, 1,* 1–4.

Smith, S. M. (1983). Disaster: Family disruption in the wake of natural disaster. In C. R. Figley & H. I. McCubbin (Eds.), *Stress and the family: Vol. 2. Coping with catastrophe* (pp. 3-20). New York: Brunner/Mazel.

Solomon, R. L., Kamin, L. F., & Wynne, L. C. (1953) Traumatic avoidance learning: The outcomes of several extinction procedures with dogs. *Journal of Abnormal and Social Psychology, 48,* 219-302.

Solomon, R. L., & Wynne, L. C. (1954). Traumatic avoidance learning: The principles of anxiety conservation and partial irreversibility. *Psychological Review, 61,* 353-385.

Stanton, D., & Figley, C. R. (1978). Treating the Vietnam veteran within the family system. In C. R. Figley (Ed.), *Stress disorders among Vietnam veterans: Theory, research, and treatment* (pp. 281-290). New York: Brunner/Mazel.

Terr, L. (1989). Treating psychic trauma in children: A preliminary discussion. *Journal of Traumatic Stress, 2*(1), 3-20.

Trimble, M. R. (1981). *Post-traumatic neurosis: From railway spine to the whiplash.* New York: Wiley.

U.S. Department of Justice, Federal Bureau of Investigation (1986). *Uniform Crime Reports for 1985.* Washington, D.C.: U.S. Government Printing Office.

Veith, I. (1965). *Hysteria: The history of a disease.* Chicago: University of Chicago Press.

Watzlawick, P., Beavin, J. H., & Jackson, D. D. (1967). *Pragmatics of human communication: A study of interactional patterns, pathologies, and paradoxes.* New York: Norton.

Watzlawick, P., Weakland, J. II., & Fisch, R. (1974). *Change: Principles of problem formation and problem resolution.* New York: Norton.

Wilson, J. P., & Krauss, G. (1985). Predicting PTSD among Vietnam veterans. In W. Kelly (Ed.), *Post-traumatic Stress Disorder and the War Veteran Patient* (pp. 102-148). New York: Brunner/Mazel.

Wolff, H. G. (1953). *Stress and disease.* S. Wolf (Ed.), Springfield, Ill.: Charles C. Thomas.

Zilbach, J. J. (1986). *Young children in family therapy.* New York: Brunner/Mazel.

Zilbach, J. (Ed.). (1989). *Children in family therapy.* New York: Haworth.

INDEX